Child Development

for Early Years Students and Practitioners

Second edition

Sally Neaum

Los Angeles | London | New Delhi
Singapore | Washington DC

Learning Matters
An imprint of SAGE Publications Ltd
1 Oliver's Yard
55 City Road
London EC1Y 1SP

SAGE Publications Inc
2455 Teller Road
Thousand Oaks, California 91320

SAGE Publications India Pvt Ltd
B 1/I 1 Mohan Cooperative Industrial Area
Mathura Road
New Delhi 11 0 044

SAGE Publications Asia-Pacific Pte Ltd
3 Church Street
#10–04 Samsung Hub
Singapore 049483

Editor: Amy Thornton
Development editor: Geoff Barker
Production controller: Chris Marke
Project management: Deer Park Productions,
                    Tavistock, Devon
Marketing manager: Catherine Slinn
Cover design: Wendy Scott
Typeset by: Pantek Media, Maidstone, Kent
Printed and bound in Great Britain by:
Henry Ling Limited, at the Dorset Press,
Dorchester, DT1 1HD

First published in 2010 by Learning Matters Ltd as
Child Development for Early Childhood Studies

Second edition published in 2013

© 2013 Sally Neaum
Reprinted 2013

Library of Congress Control Number: 2013932595

British Library Cataloguing in Publication Data

A catalogue record for this book is available from the
British Library

ISBN: 978 1 44626 752 3 (hbk) and
ISBN: 978 1 44626 753 0 (pbk)

Child Development

for Early Years Students and Practitioners

Second edition

Contents

Section 1: Early childhood context and policy

Section 2: Children's development

Section 3: Applying child development in practice

Section 4: Enhancing practice and understanding

The author

Sally Neaum is a lecturer in Early Childhood, and teaches primary English in initial teacher training. She has worked as a nursery and primary school teacher, as an advisor in early years and inclusion. She has an M.Ed in Educational Psychology and Special Educational Needs and her doctoral research was in the pedagogy of early literacy.

Acknowledgements

The author and publisher would like to thank the following for permission to reproduce copyright material: SAGE and Nelson Thornes publishers and my co-authors, Jill Tallack, Marion Beaver and Jo Brewster, as well as Anning and Ball, for permission to use material from our books.

Every effort has been made to trace the copyright holders and to obtain their permission for the use of copyright material. The publisher and author will gladly receive any information enabling them to rectify any error or omission in subsequent editions.

Introduction

This book is about children's development and learning. The focus is on understanding both the developmental patterns and sequences in children's development and how the context of this learning impacts on children's progress. Knowing about children and their development underpins all that we do in early years. It enables people who live and work with very young children to interact with them in an appropriate way and to provide developmentally appropriate experiences to support their development. Knowing about child development also enables us to identify children who may need additional support to enable them to maintain developmental progress and to learn.

This book is divided into four sections:

- understanding the context of children's development;
- understanding children's development;
- child development in practice;
- enhancing practice and understanding.

Section 1: Early childhood context and policy
Chapter 1: Children and childhood: a historical perspective

This chapter explores how our understandings of children and childhood have changed over time according to the moral, ethical and political choices that we have made within society. To illustrate this there are examples of the differences in the experience of children across time and cultures. The chapter also explores our current conceptualisation of what it means to be a child in our society. You are asked to consider the complexity of our current understanding of children and childhood by considering how we talk, write and think about children in our society. Pen portraits of influential early years thinkers, theories and pioneers are outlined.

Chapter 2: The current policy context of early years

This chapter identifies and explains the important policies, practice frameworks and workforce development initiatives in the field of early years. The chapter outlines the evidence regarding young children's learning and development that underpins policy, practice and workforce development.

Section 2: Children's development
Chapter 3: Holistic development

'Holistic' is a term that is often used about young children's learning and development. This chapter outlines what is meant by holistic development and gives an example of how the nature of young children's play remains holistic however we as adults choose to deconstruct, label and categorise what young children do. It also addresses how we ensure that at all levels of provision we acknowledge and provide for the holistic nature of young children's learning.

Chapter 4: Children's development

This chapter outlines developmental sequences and progress across all aspects of young children's learning. It starts with the principles of development and then outlines expected developmental parameters, between birth and seven years old, in the areas of physical development, cognitive (intellectual) development, linguistic development and emotional and social development.

Chapter 5: Development in the Early Years Foundation Stage

The EYFS (2012) is the statutory framework that all funded early years providers must work within. This chapter outlines the ways in which development is understood in the EYFS and the requirements for practitioners to make assessments of children's developmental progress towards a series of stated learning goals. The role and expectations of practitioners in providing for young children's development and learning is outlined.

Chapter 6: Factors affecting children's learning and development

This chapter identifies and explains the factors that are known to affect children's learning and development. It explores the question of why it is that some children, and some identifiable groups of children, consistently fall outside of expected developmental parameters. The chapter explores the importance of providing for all children's learning and development both as a moral and political choice within our society and as inclusive practice.

Section 3: Applying child development in practice

Chapter 7: Supporting children's learning and development

If children are to learn and develop well it is important that practitioners, parents and carers understand how children learn and how to interact with children to best support this learning. This chapter outlines learning theory that articulates how young children learn, including the importance of language in learning, and the pedagogical practices that support children's learning. The significance of the home environment in children's learning and development is acknowledged and the initiatives to support parents to enable them to understand their child's development and their role in supporting it are identified.

Chapter 8: Observing and assessing children's learning and development

This chapter looks at why we observe and assess young children's learning. It outlines what we can observe and assess, and how to do this. The distinction is made between formative and summative assessment and this is related to early years practice. The requirement for observation-based assessment in the EYFS is highlighted.

Section 4: Enhancing practice and understanding

Chapter 9: Reflecting on children's learning and development

This chapter introduces the idea of reflective practice as an important professional skill. It outlines the process of reflection and explains how reflective practice supports children's learning and development. The importance of the reflective process in developing our own understandings of what constitutes effective early years practice is emphasised.

Chapter 10: Thinking, questioning and challenging: a critical approach to the early years

This is a completely new chapter since the first edition of this book (previously entitled *Child Development for Early Childhood Studies*). This chapter encourages you to adopt a critical approach to early years. By critical we mean a thoughtful, analytical and evaluative approach. The chapter explores why this is important and offers some examples of a critical approach in the early years. It also encourages you to think carefully about assumptions that we may make when we talk about child development. Clearly there is a substantial body of professional knowledge and skill that early years practitioners need to acquire and it is important to learn this. However, it is just as important to think carefully about what you know and what you do to ensure that your professional knowledge and skills are not just *acquired* knowledge but *considered* knowledge.

Section 1

Early childhood context and policy

1 Children and childhood: a historical perspective

This chapter enables you to understand:

- different concepts of children and childhood through history;
- the nature–nurture debate in child development;
- our current understandings of children and childhood;
- child development as a combination of observable biological development and social experience within a specific social, cultural and historical context;
- the importance of seeing child development in a holistic way;
- how to be critically aware of the conceptualisation of children in literature, reports and frameworks associated with children and childhood.

Introduction

Have you ever thought about what it means when we talk about children or childhood? What is your understanding of what it means to be a child or have a childhood? What is child development? Where have these understandings come from? How do these understandings influence approaches to children? Consideration of these issues will allow Early Years practitioners to engage in critical thinking about current concepts of children and childhood and how they influence our thinking and practice. This chapter will enable you to understand different ways of seeing children and childhood and explore how this informs our current understanding of child development.

Through the nineteenth and twentieth centuries there has been a series of changes of focus in our understandings and perceptions of children and childhood. Academic disciplines such as science, medicine, psychology and sociology, and changes in the influence of faith in society, have had a powerful influence over how society is constructed. Concepts of children and childhood are part of these changes and re-conceptualisations.

The frameworks that determine understandings of children and childhood are ethical and political choices made within wider ideas, values and rationalities of a society (Moss and Petrie, 2002). These ethical and political choices determine what each society will construct as what it means to be a child and to experience childhood within that society at that point in history. As these ethical and political frameworks develop and change it is very likely that understandings of children and childhood within each society will also develop and change.

Alan Prout (2005) traces these changes through the nineteenth and twentieth centuries. He observes that, with regard to children and childhood, there has been a shift in both intellectual processes and material practices. Prout (2005) highlights the significant shifts in our understandings of children and childhood which have come together to form our current conceptualisation of what it means to be a child in our society.

The concept of childhood: an overview

In medieval times children, once they were weaned, were regarded as little adults. There was no distinct phase of life known or understood as childhood. Hugh Cunningham observes that childhood was not thought to be as important as we now consider it in the formation of personality and character. The predominant social force was the church whose focus was upon the baptism – to free the child from original sin and receive them into the church. Children were regarded as imperfect and sinful and their upbringing usually reflected these harsh beliefs.

From the seventeenth century, in Western countries, a different concept of childhood began to emerge. This was heavily influenced by the work of the philosopher John Locke (1632–1704) whose ideas about learning and education suggested that there were differences between adults and children. Locke's work is characterised by his opposition to authoritarianism. He wanted individuals to use reason to search after truth rather than unquestionably accept the opinion of authorities, including the church, or rely on superstition. One of Locke's most influential ideas was that we are all born as blank slates (*tabula rasa*), that we have no innate knowledge but we acquire what we know after we are born through sensation and reflection. Similarly the ideas of philosopher Jean Jacques Rousseau (1712–1778) were highly influential in encouraging thinking about what is meant to be a child and how children learn and grow and develop. Rousseau proposed that we were all born essentially good and innocent; therefore children should be loved, nurtured and protected. Education, he believed, would support this process by cultivating the good in people. Both philosophers' ideas challenged the notion of original sin and began the process of a different way of thinking about children and childhood. These shifts and changes in our understandings of children and childhood have continued through to the present day.

ACTIVITY 1

- *What is meant by original sin?*

- *How did this influence the view of children in society?*

Find out more about the work of Locke and Rousseau.

- *How did their ideas of challenge existing understandings of childhood?*

- *What impact do you think this had on how children were perceived in society?*

- *What is you view on these different conceptualisations of children?*

Children, childhood and modernity

From the eighteenth century onwards there were profound political, economic, technological, social and cultural changes in societies throughout Europe. Societies were changing from predominantly rural agricultural-based societies to ones based on industrial capitalism. The move was strongly influenced by advances in science and technology. These advances precipitated a strong belief in the power of the scientific and technological as a way to understand and control the world, including ourselves. Within this context, encouraged by the work of Charles Darwin, emerged the Child Study Movement. Its aim was to highlight the role of the biological processes in human development. Their approach was scientific: the belief in, and use of, testing, observation and experimentation to discover universal laws expressed as theory. The movement demonstrated, and popularised, the view that children's conception and mental processes differed from those of adults. This supported the conceptualisation of childhood as a different and distinct stage of life from adulthood. Children were conceptualised as being in a more primitive stage of development than adults both biologically and socially. The development of children therefore became an area for scientific study and understanding, the outcomes of which, it was hoped, would identify focused interventions that would shape and mould children's lives.

Paediatric medicine and child psychology

Prout (2005) identifies two important disciplines that strongly influenced the Child Study Movement and focused attention on the biological aspects of being a child: the development of the science of paediatric medicine and the child psychology movement.

Paediatric medicine

The development of the discipline of paediatric medicine was an important part of the rise of the scientific study of children. The understanding of childhood disease as a separate branch of medicine became formalised in 1901 by the foundation of the Society for the Study of Diseases of Children. A medical model of children and childhood, in which children's development can be measured, monitored and managed, thus became part of our conceptualisation of children.

Child psychology

Alongside paediatrics a discipline emerging from the Child Study Movement was the development of child psychology. Prout (2005) argues that there were multiple strands of research and investigation that came together to support the understanding of children and their development, namely: the work of Skinner on behaviourism; Bowlby's work on attachment; Freud and psychoanalysis; the work of Piaget and the cognitive psychology movement; and an emerging understanding of language development.

These psychological understandings came together to create a discipline of child psychology. In this emerging discipline children were examined and tested in order to identify 'normal' ranges of functioning and behaviour that were defined and named. These assertions of what constitutes normal functioning also created the potential for defining abnormal and pathological behaviour (Prout, 2005). This 'abnormal' functioning became the site for intervention and a range of professions developed around identifying children who would benefit from intervention, for example, educational psychology. These psychological frameworks for understanding child development quickly became part of a general understanding of children and childhood. The language of psychology such as 'stages of development,' 'attachment' and 'bonding' entered everyday talk and practice via the work of child-rearing gurus such as Dr Benjamin Spock (Prout, 2005). At this stage in its development child psychology was predominantly informed by a biological view of child development; children and childhood were viewed as universal constants. The approach was to think about the individual child without consideration of the context of their social world. Within this discipline, development, whether typical or atypical, was regarded as a 'within-child' phenomenon and explanations sought through theories developed within a scientific and/or medical framework.

The emergence of a social model of childhood

Toward the end of the twentieth century there was growing criticism of how child psychology conceptualised childhood (Prout, 2005). The concern centred on a increasing awareness of, and sensitivity to, the social context of behaviour. Prout (2005, p.51) observes that *at the centre of this critical approach was the notion that children are shaped by their different social contexts and that this cannot be left out of the psychological account.*

He cites the work of Bronfenbrenner and Vygotsky as having particular importance in the emergence of a social model of childhood. The work of Bronfenbrenner and Vygotsky, and others, moved the debate about children's development away from the emphasis on child development purely as an inevitable biological unfolding towards an understanding that development occurs through the interplay of biology and social experience.

THEORY FOCUS

Urie Bronfenbrenner (1917–2005)

Bronfenbrenner developed a model that focused on the importance of both biological factors and the social environment in children's development. He proposed that whilst a child's biological development unfolds there is also a complex pattern of interaction with people and social patterns, institutions, and the environment around the child that similarly influences child development. Bronfenbrenner's work began to reframe the understanding of children, away from the ideas that children and childhood are universal constants that can be observed and defined in a scientific model, and towards a more complex view of children and childhood. This view recognised that childhood was experienced differently by different children in different societies. So, whilst it could be observed that many biological factors remained similar across different societies, differences in children and the experience of childhood were because of their social experiences. Bronfenbrenner's ecology of human development is outlined in Chapter 2.

THEORY FOCUS

Lev Vygotsky (1896–1924)

Lev Vygotsky's work, similar to that of Bronfenbrenner, emphasised the importance of the social in children's development. He argued that it is through others that we become ourselves. The main premise of his work is the interrelationship between thought and language. Language, he argues, forms the basis of thought. Language development is dependent on the child's social cultural experience and is also the primary tool by which we learn. In this way rich and effective language, developed in a social context, is vital to children's development and shapes the developing child.

The impact of these changes on the way society and its institutions are constructed was, and continues to be, profound. All of our everyday lives, particularly those of us who work with young children, have been affected by these shifts and changes in our understanding of children and childhood.

The nature–nurture debate

The nature–nurture debate is one about the relative importance of biology and social experience in who we are and who we become.

Nature refers to our biology – the genetically programmed process of physical maturation. Nurture refers to all the experiences we have after we are born that influence who we are and what we know.

The medical and scientific view of child development emphasises nature, and a social model of child development emphasises nurture. The current understanding is that both are significant in children's growth and development. This reflects the historical shifts and changes in our views of children and childhood. What is now understood is that child development, in all areas of learning, is a complex combination of children's biological maturational processes and their social experiences. For example, children are born with the potential for developing language. It is innate (nature). However, other aspects of language development, such as the rate of development, the sophistication of a child's language skill and his or her individual accent and vocabulary are determined by inter-active experiences after birth (nurture). This interplay between nature and nurture is different in different areas of development; for example, biological maturation plays a greater part in physical development than in social and emotional development. Beaver (1994) shows the relative influences of nature and nurture across the areas of child development. It is important to remember that these are relative influences; there is no definitive understanding of the relative impact of nature and nurture in the different areas of child development. See Figure 1.1:

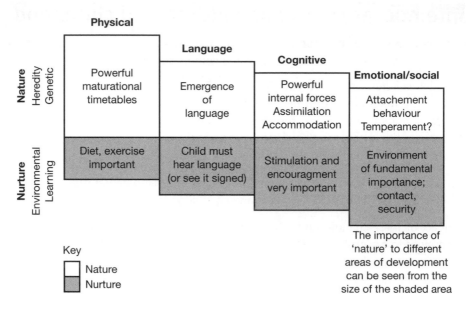

Figure 1.1 Chart showing the relative influence of nature and nurture on different developmental areas

---

CASE STUDY

Esme is a talented flautist. Her mother is also an excellent flautist. Esme's mum used to play her flute to her as a baby and toddler. Esme loved listening to the flute and they would enjoy times together. As she got older Esme was taken to 'music makers', a music group for toddlers where she developed a wider awareness of music. Esme's mum taught her the basics of flute playing whilst she was still very young and when she was old enough she began lessons with a teacher. Esme and her mum practise most evenings and really enjoy playing together.

ACTIVITY 2

- *How much of Esme's ability is innate talent?*

- *What, if anything, do you think she inherited from her mother?*

- *How much of her talent comes from her experiences, for example, exposure to music at home, at music groups and lessons, regular focused practice, modelled behaviour and encouragement from her family and teacher?*

- *What does this tell you about the interplay of nature and nurture in what we know and can do?*

- *What are the implications of these different views for how we think about and organise provision in society for children?*

Contemporary views of children and childhood

The impact of historical shifts and changes in what we know about children's development and how it is viewed within the social and cultural context has resulted in a complex pattern of contemporary understandings of children and childhood. Both a biological and a social model of children and childhood are evident in contemporary understandings.

The biological child of child development

Work in the disciplines of science, psychology, sociology and education has enabled us to have a good understanding of development, including developmental sequences. Clearly this knowledge has application in understanding children's development, including atypical development, and in informing aspects of intervention.

Child development patterns and charts are used throughout childhood to inform the work of professionals who work with children; for example, babies are offered a series of developmental checks in which their progress in mapped against typical development. This enables babies to be screened for possible congenital abnormalities, emerging behavioural difficulties and developmental delays.

This, in its purest form, is a view of children and childhood as a series of unfolding biological states. The focus is on the individual child who follows a predetermined series of developmental stages that are biologically determined. Child development is thus regarded as observable, measurable and quantifiable (Moss and Petrie, 2002). Where development is assessed as atypical interventions can be applied with the aim of supporting children's development, and, where possible, bringing it back within the parameters of developmental expectations.

Childhood development as a social construction

> *Childhood does not exist – we create it as a society.*
> (Rinaldi, 1999, in Moss and Petrie, 2002, p.20)

This is a different understanding of children and childhood. This understanding regards childhood as being socially constructed. That is, that our understandings of what it means to be a child are created within society. What childhood means will therefore be different in different societies and at different times in history. This view does not challenge the notion that there are some observable stages of development in childhood but recognises the limitation of a biological approach to development in exploring what childhood means within each society and how children experience it.

Childhoods within their historical, social and cultural contexts

These case studies show how different children's experiences of childhood can be because of when and where they were born. These understandings and expectations of young children are created within each society's historical and cultural context. They are different because different societies' expectations about what constitutes childhood are different.

Victorian children

In Victorian times many poor children worked in mills, mines, as servants and on the streets. Tony Robinson (2005) in his book entitled *The worst children's jobs in history* describes their lives. The jobs that came out of the Industrial Revolution made Britain one of the richest nations in the world. Men invented machines that made complicated work so easy even a child could do it – and tens of thousands of them did just that.

CASE STUDY

Elizabeth is six years old and works in a cotton mill. Her day starts at 5.30 a.m. and she works until 8 p.m. The cotton mill is a very scary place. Huge machines made of wood and metal clatter, rattle, swish, bang, whirr, thud and clunk away all day. They make some people very rich but not Elizabeth and the other children who worked there ... for them they are hellish places.

Elizabeth works on the spinning mule. The spinning mule spins cotton thread much faster than a spinning wheel could. Elizabeth works as a piecer. She sticks any broken bits of cotton together while the mule is moving. In order to do this she has to spit on the ends and twist them backwards and forwards which makes her fingers bleed. She isn't allowed to sit down while she is working. The machine moves right across the room and back as it winds the thread on the bobbins and Elizabeth has to walk alongside it without stopping. Each day at work she walks about 20 miles.

While the mule is spinning and Elizabeth is piecing, bits of cotton fluff drift under the machines. These have to be cleared because they could start a fire. The easiest way to do this is for one of the smallest children to crawl under the machine with a brush. This has to be done whilst the machine is working. These children are called scavengers and Elizabeth has seen many get their heads, arms, legs, hands and toes crushed by the moving machinery.

Adapted from Robinson (2005)

Yanomamo people

Napoleon Chagnon spent 19 months living with, and completing an anthropological study of, the Yanomamo people. The Yanomamo lived in a remote part of Venezuela and northern Brazil. When Chagnon completed the study between 1964 and 1966 most of the villages had never had any contact with outsiders. Criticisms have been levelled at Chagnon's study, however, these were for interpretive and ethical reasons (Borofsky, 2005), not his descriptions of the lives of the people. Chagnon (1968) describes below what he observed about the daily activities of Yanomamo children.

CASE STUDY

Kaobawa spends a great deal of time exploring the wonders of the plant and animal life around him and is an accomplished botanist. At twelve years of age he can name 20 species of bees and give the anatomical or behavioural reasons for their distinctions. Bahimi, an eight-year-old girl, brought me a tiny egg-like structure on one occasion and asked me to watch it with her. Presently it cracked open and numerous baby cockroaches poured out, while she described the intimate details of the reproductive process to me.

The younger children stay close to their mothers but the older ones have considerable freedom to wander about the garden (the planted areas around the village centre) at play. Ariwari and his friends hunt for lizards with miniature bows and feathers. If they catch one alive they bring it back to the village and tie a string around it. The string is anchored to a stick in the village clearing and Ariwari and his friends chase it gleefully, shooting scores of tiny arrows at it. Since lizards are quick and the boys poor shots the target practice can last for hours.

The young girls' experience is different. Bahimi and her friends soon learn that it is a man's world for they must assume much of the responsibility for tending their younger siblings, hauling water and fire wood, and in general helping their busy mothers.

Adapted from Chagnon (1968)

ACTIVITY 3

Read through the two case studies of children's lives above.

How do they demonstrate that children's lives are socially and culturally determined by where and when they grow up?

What are the social and cultural contexts that have been shown to impact on children's lives in our society?

In what ways can these contexts impact on children's lives?

In what ways do we, in our provision for children, aim to ensure that all children have a chance to fulfil their potential?

Considering contemporary childhood

Understandings of children and childhood that inform current discussion and debate are based on a wide range of social, cultural and biological understandings of children and childhood. These understandings are not necessarily cohesive because they have been formed and patterned over time from a variety of influences. These understandings come together to form complex, sometimes competing, views of children and childhood in contemporary society (Dahlberg, Moss and Pence, 1999; Moss and Petrie, 2002).

Representations of what we believe about children in contemporary society are evident in what we read and the frameworks we use for children. These representations can reveal the complex understandings that we have built about children and childhood.

Read these different conceptualisations of children and childhood that are evident in literature, reports and frameworks associated with children. Consider what they reveal about contemporary understandings of children and childhood.

1 A good childhood (Layard and Dunn, 2009)

In many ways our children have never lived so well. Materially they have more possessions, better homes, more holidays away. They enjoy a whole world of technology which brings them music, information, entertainment and an unprecedented ability to communicate. Our children are also more educated and sick less often than before. They are more open and honest about themselves and more tolerant of human diversity in all its forms. And they are more concerned about the environment. And yet there is also widespread unease about our children's experience – that somehow their lives are becoming more difficult. The report showed how children are faring in all 21 of the world's richest countries. It began with an overall ranking of the 21 countries ... Britain came bottom of the class.

2 How could any child do this to another?

By Claire Lewis
Crime reporter

Two violent young brothers aged ten and twelve could be locked up for life after admitting one of the most serious and shocking crimes South Yorkshire has ever suffered.

The pair lured two little boys – an uncle and nephew aged 11 and nine, who were cycling to a pond to go fishing – to wasteland where they promised to show them a strange animal they had found. Instead they attacked them. Ian Wright, aged 40, who found the older victim face-down and left for dead at the foot of a ravine, branded the torturers 'animals'. 'They're animals, absolute animals,' he said. 'How any child could do this to another child I don't know.'

www.thestar.co.uk/news/39How-any-child-could-do.5618181.jp?CommentPage=2&CommentPageLength=10#comments

3 Declaration of the Rights of the Child

Proclaimed by General Assembly resolution 1386(XIV) of 20 November 1959

Principle 2
The child shall enjoy *special protection*, and shall be given opportunities and facilities, by law and by other means, to enable him to develop physically, mentally, morally, spiritually and socially in a healthy and normal manner and in conditions of freedom and dignity.

4 Reggio Emilia

The work of the Reggio Emilia schools in Italy has been highly influential in shaping Early Years education in Britain. Pre-school provision in Reggio Emilia is based upon an understanding of children who are active authors of their own lives, influential in others' lives and in shaping society. The child is understood as being *rich in potential, strong, powerful, competent, and most of all, connected to adults and other children* (Malaguzzi, 1993, p.75).

5 DFE (2012) Statutory Framework for the Early Years Foundation

Foundation Stage Principles – A unique child. Every child is a unique child who is constantly learning and can be resilient, capable, confident and self-assured.

6 Child growth chart

(See Figure 1.2)

7 Diagnostic criteria for Rett's disorder

(A)
All of the following:

- apparently normal prenatal and perinatal development

- apparently normal psychomotor development through the first five months after birth

- normal head circumference at birth.

(B)
Onset of all of the following after the period of normal development:

- deceleration of head growth between ages 5 and 48 months

- loss of previously acquired purposeful hand skills between ages 5 and 30 months with the subsequent development of stereotyped hand movements (e.g., hand-wringing or hand washing)

- loss of social engagement early in the course (although often social interaction develops later)

- appearance of poorly coordinated gait or trunk movements

- severely impaired expressive and receptive language development with severe psychomotor retardation.

Diagnostic and Statistical Manual of Mental Disorders: DSM IV published by the American Psychiatric Society

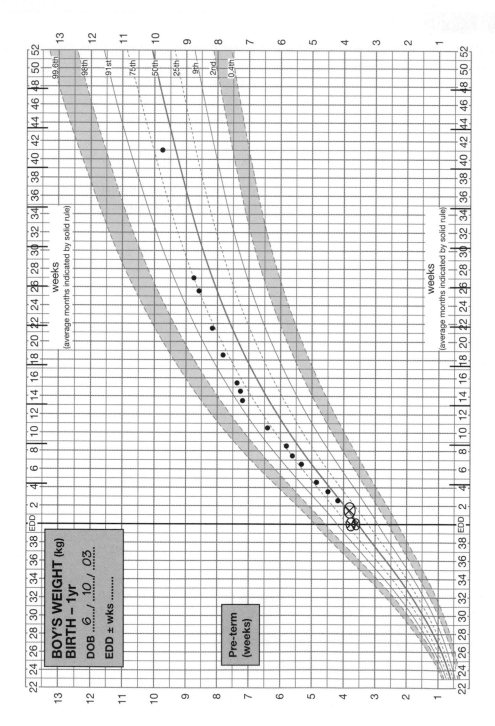

Figure 1.2 A sample child growth chart

ACTIVITY 4

- *What is the understanding of a child and/or childhood in each example?*

- *Think about the interplay of the biological and the social in child development. Which is emphasised in each example? Why do you think that this is?*

- *Taken together what do they tell you about the current conceptualisation of children and childhood?*

- *What are the implications of this for early years practitioners?*

- *Look at the development matters section of the Early Years Foundation Stage. Where can you find evidence of these different ways of conceptualising children and early childhood?*

It is important that early years practitioners working with children and families are aware of all the different ways in which society constructs children and childhood and how this is reflected in the ways in which we think about, talk and write about, and assess children. We need to ensure that we are careful to see children in a holistic way recognising that children's development is a complex combination of observable patterns of development embedded in the context of children's social and cultural environment, and that their experiences within that context will be highly influential in who they are and what they can do.

Early years theorists, thinkers and pioneers

In addition to a wide range of societal and cultural influences, such as medical and social models development, our understanding of children and early childhood has been influenced by a number of individual theorists, thinkers and pioneers. These people developed particular views on children and childhood which were both influenced by and helped to shape wider cultural and societal understandings. Their ideas have come together to influence and inform our current understandings of children and childhood.

These theorists, thinkers and pioneers were not a cohesive group of people working together. They came from different disciplines, they worked in different ways, in different countries, at different times and focused on different aspects of children and childhood. What they all had in common was a desire to understand children and childhood; how children grow and learn and, for some, the ways in which society should provide for and support this development. Their ideas have had a significant impact on our current understanding of children and childhood and their work is continued today in research as we strive to understand how children grow and learn and how best to support this.

The pen portraits below present these people's main ideas.

Theorists
These people developed and articulated a theory about a particular aspect of children's learning and development. Their work is outlined in more detail throughout this book. This chart highlights their main contribution to our understanding of young children's learning and development.
Jean Piaget (1896–1980) Swiss developmental psychologist A staged outline of children's cognitive development.
John Bowlby (1907–1990) British psychologist, psychiatrist and psychoanalyst Attachment theory.
Lev Vygotsky (1896–1934) Russian psychologist The social dimension of children's learning Zone of Proximal Development The relationship between speech and language and conceptual development.
Jerome Bruner (1915–) American psychologist Learning as an active rather than passive process Scaffolding – The role of others in children's learning Social interactionist theory of language development.
Urie Bronfenbrenner (1917–2005) American psychologist Ecology of human development – the socially embedded nature of children's learning and development.

Table 1.1 Theorists

Thinkers and pioneers
These people articulated ideas about children and childhood and their growth and development that enabled us to further understand how children think and learn. Some made direct links between their ideas and provision for children.
John Locke (1638–1704) Philosopher Suggested that there were differences between the way adults and children think and learn. Argued that children were born as blank sheets (*tabula rasa*) and that we learn everything through the experiences that we have after we are born.
Jean-Jacques Rousseau (1712–1778) Philosopher, composer and writer Rousseau looked to nature as inspiration for his theory on human nature. His most famous work on childhood and education is *Emile; or, On Education*. He argues that education should be concerned with developing a child's character and moral sense so that he/she is able to remain virtuous in the unnatural and imperfect social society. He was an early advocate of developmentally appropriate education and the importance of understanding the consequences of action rather than punishment in learning right from wrong. He advocated that children learned through direct experience in the natural world.
Friedrich Froebel (1782–1852) German thinker and educator Best known for his insight that the first early learning experiences of the very young are of crucial importance in influencing their later education and therefore the health and development of society as a whole. He devised a set of principles that underpinned an interactive learning process and set up settings where this could take place. He named settings for young children 'kindergarten' (children's garden): a place where children can be nourished.

Robert Owen (1771–1825) Social reformer
Owen endeavoured to improve the health, education and well-being of working people. He was instrumental in developing a model community set up in the mill town of Lanark in Scotland. The community provided education for all children including an infant school, a crèche for working mothers, free medical care and evening classes and leisure activities for adults. Children were not allowed to work in the mill until the age of ten. This was a radical departure from existing ways that children and workers were treated in the mills. His work had an impact in the development of infant education, humane working practices and trade unionism.

Rachel Macmillan (1859–1917), Margaret Macmillan (1860–1931) Socialist reformers
Rachel and Margaret Macmillan were social reformers concerned with the link between the physical environment and intellectual development. They led campaigns to improve the well-being of industrial workers, and they supported the suffragette movement. In their work with children they emphasised the importance of physical health in a child's development. They campaigned for school meals for children living in poverty, they opened the country's first school clinic to improve children's health and provided a Night Camp where children living in slums could wash and wear clean nightclothes. The sisters stressed the importance of fresh air and play outdoors for young children and so in 1914, in accordance with these beliefs, they opened an open-air nursery and training centre in London.

Susan Issacs (1885–1948) Psychoanalyst and teacher
Susan Issacs' radical approach to education was evident in her Malting House School. Her educational philosophy saw all children as able and willing to learn given the right environment for learning. Issacs' Malting House school didn't follow a traditional curriculum, instead children were free to follow their curiosity and interest in a rich environment that included woodworking areas, a large garden, and chemistry lab. She observed the children learning and adapted her interaction and approach to meet their needs. This child-centred approach to education has been highly influential in the development of current Early Years practice.

Maria Montessori (1870–1952) Italian medical doctor who became a professor of pedagogy at the University of Rome
Montessori's work focused on women's rights and social reform. Within this she developed an innovative approach to the education of young children – the Montessori method. The approach is underpinned by the belief that children are profoundly affected by society and by their immediate environment. It holds that all children have the potential and drive to learn and that mixed aged groups and freedom to work and explore their environment facilitate this potential. The approach requires specially prepared child-centred environments called children's houses. These children's houses include specifically designed materials that enable them to develop social and intellectual capabilities. The approach emphasises the importance of the child exploring the environment with the adults acting as observers, only intervening on the periphery and only when necessary.

Rudolph Steiner (1861–1925) Austrian philosopher
Steiner developed the idea of Anthroposophy. He believed that we build a healthy society by focusing on the material, soul and spiritual needs of human beings. Steiner described three major developmental stages in child development that extend from early childhood to adolescence. His engagement with schools and schooling arose from a lecture that he gave at the Waldorf-Astoria cigarette factory in 1919 that resulted in the opening of a school based on the his views. Steiner/Waldorf schools are now worldwide. Their stated aim is to provide an unhurried and creative learning experience where children find joy in childhood and in their learning, in contrast to early specialism or a strong academic focus. The curriculum is a flexible set of guidelines that take account of all aspects of a child's learning, working in harmony with the different phases of child development. Collaborative learning is encouraged and there is a strong emphasis on the arts, including *Eurythmy* – an expressive movement art performed in response to the spoken word and music.

Elinor Goldschmeid (1910–2009) Early years educator
Goldschmeid contributed a number of ideas to the field based on her experiences working with very young children in Italy and London. Her significant contributions include treasure baskets, heuristic play and the key person system. All of these are now regarded as important aspects of Nursery provision for young children.

continued

Thinkers and pioneers These people articulated ideas about children and childhood and their growth and development that enabled us to further understand how children think and learn. Some made direct links between their ideas and provision for children.

Margaret Donaldson (1926–) Developmental psychologist

Donaldson was working at a time when the predominant view of children's learning was behaviourist. She challenged this notion arguing that children were active in trying to understand and pattern meaning from things that they are asked to do. She used the terms embedded and disembedded thinking. Embedded thinking is thinking that has a context that makes sense to the child. In contrast disembedded thinking is when tasks have no familiar or realistic context for the child to engage with and thus are difficult to make sense of. To achieve this Donaldson recognised the importance of seeing and presenting things from a child's point of view, decentering from an adult perception of the world. She also stressed the importance of focusing on what children can do rather than what they cannot do.

Chris Athey (1924–2011)

Chris Athey developed the notion of 'schemas' in young children's learning. Schemeas, she argued, are means of learning classifications and categories. They are cognitive structures that develop initially through motor action and symbolisation to support thinking. They are built on and put together over time to create detailed and powerful higher-level schemas. She developed her ideas through close observation of children's drawing and painting. She argues that the schemas that children are interested in and are evident in their artwork are similarly evident in their play as children explore and represent their thinking. Observing and identifying schema is used in many Early Years settings as a way of analysing and providing appropriately for children's learning.

Professor Ferre Laevers

Laevers' team at the Research Centre for Experimental Education in Leuven, Belgium, developed the Leuven Scale for observing and assessing children's well-being and involvement. It was developed in response to the question of what constitutes quality in early care and education. The team believe that quality is determined by the degree of emotional well-being and involvement that the children experience, and argue that deep learning will occur when children have high levels of involvement and well-being.

Table 1.2 Thinkers and pioneers

C H A P T E R   S U M M A R Y

In this chapter we have considered the historical concepts of children and childhood and how this informs contemporary understandings. Through the case studies we can see that different children experience childhood differently because of the social, cultural and historical context of their childhood. We have seen how current understandings of child development have been patterned over time to include both biological and social aspects of development and how this is reflected in the nature–nurture debate in child development. The work of different theorist, thinkers and pioneers has been outlined and identified as important in shaping our ideas. By looking at some different ways in which children are written about and assessed we can see how our current understandings of children and childhood are complex. From this we have concluded that it is important to see children and child development holistically; that child development is both a biological maturational unfolding and a consequence of the context in which the child grows up.

FURTHER READING

Beaver, M (1994) *Babies and young children development 0–7.* Cheltenham: Nelson Thornes.

Borofsky, R (2005) *Yanomani: the fierce controversy and what we can learn from it.* University of California Press.

Burr, V (1995) *An introduction to social constructionism.* London: Routledge.

Chagnon, N (1968) *Yanomamo. The fierce people.* New York: Holt Reinhart Winston.

Cunningham, H http://open2.net/theinventionofchildhood/childhood_inventions.html

Dahlberg, G, Moss, P and Pence, P (1999) *Beyond quality in early childhood and care. Postmodern perspectives.* London: Falmer Books.

DFE (2012) Statutory Framework for the Early Years Foundation Stage. DFE. **https://www.education. gov.uk/publications/standard/publicationDetail/Page1/DFE-00023-2012**

Guldberg, H (2009) *Reclaiming childhood. Freedom and play in an age of fear.* London: Routledge.

James, A and Prout, A (1997) *Constructing and reconstructing childhood. Contemporary issues in the sociological study of childhood.* London: RoutledgeFalmer.

Layard, R and Dunn, J (2009) *A good childhood. Searching for values in a competitive age.* London: Penguin Books.

Malaguzzi, L (1993) History, ideas and basic philosophy. In Edwards, C, Gandidi, L and Forman, G *The hundred languages of children.* New Jersey: Ablex Publishing Corporation.

Moss, P and Petrie, P (2002) *From children's services to children's spaces: public policy, children and childhood.* London: RoutledgeFalmer.

Prout, A (2005) *The future of childhood.* London: RoutledgeFalmer.

Pugh, G and Duffy, B (2006) *Contemporary issues in the early years.* London: Sage.

Robinson, T (2005) *The worst children's jobs in history.* London: Pan.

2 The current policy context of early years

This chapter enables you to understand:

- the political context of early tears policy;
- the important policies, legislation, practice frameworks and workforce development in early years;
- how these policies and frameworks are informed by research into the best ways to support children's early development;
- SureStart and SureStart local programmes;
- Every Child Matters framework;
- children's centres;
- How the Early Years Professional Status has been developed to support children's early learning and development.

Introduction

From the late 1990s onwards there was an unprecedented political focus on education; this included education and care for pre-school aged children. The Labour Party, who came to power in 1997, made it one of their priorities to increase support for young children and their families.

To achieve this there were significant changes in the way that early years was funded, organised delivered and monitored. Government policy and legislation, supported by practice guidance and workforce development, reshaped early years provision. The government's aim was threefold, namely:

- to meet the early educational needs of young children;

- to meet families' needs for childcare;

- to provide wide-ranging support for parents and families.

The change to a coalition government in 2010 has inevitably meant that there have been changes in emphasis and approach to early childhood. However, the fundamental aims of supporting the early educational needs of young children and the recognition that to achieve this the government must support families has remained in place.

Policy and legislation, frameworks for practice and workforce development

Governmental policy needs to be supported by policy statements. Policy statements say what the government intends to do. These are sometimes published as, and called, Green Papers or White Papers. Green Papers are documents in which the government set out their ideas for discussion or consultation. A White Paper contains policy proposals. Policy becomes law through the passing of legislation in Parliament. Once the legislation has passed through Parliament it is called an 'act,' for example, the Disability Discrimination Act. One part of policy and legislation is to ensure that workforce training and qualifications are sufficient to put the policy into practice. Therefore, both policy and legislation often establish routes for training and qualifications within a sector. Both policy and legislation are often supported by guidance and frameworks that may state the legal requirements and offer advice on how to enact the requirements in practice and provision.

Since the 1990s there have been a large number of policies, legislation and practice guidance in early years. Detailed in Table 2.1 is a timeline of the most influential policies and guidance between 1998 and 2012.

	Policy and legislation	Practice: reports and guidance	Workforce development
1998	Children Act		
1992	Education Act – • established OFSTED – Office for Standards in Education		First degree level course in childhood studies – Suffolk College and the University of Bristol
1995	Disability Discrimination Act (DDA) this applied to all providers of Early Years services from 2002		
1996	Nursery Education and Grant Maintained Schools Act – • Introduces OFSTED inspections for nurseries • puts in place new system for funding early years – the nursery voucher scheme – initially for four year olds	Desirable Outcomes for children's learning on entering compulsory education published. The basis for inspection in early childhood education and care	
1997	Labour manifesto – focuses on reduction of child poverty and expansion of childcare and other services for children and families	Effective Provision of Pre-school Education (EPPE) study started at the Institute of Education	Fifteen early childhood degree courses available in October 1997
1999	SureStart trailblazers set up in 60 disadvantaged areas. Surestart local programmes introduced		
2000		Curriculum Guidance for the Foundation Stage replaced the Desirable Outcomes framework	

continued

	Policy and legislation	Practice: reports and guidance	Workforce development
2001		Special Educational Needs code of practice	Early years sector endorsed Foundation Degree
2002	Education Act • Nursery education to be inspected by OFSTED • Foundation Stage profile to be competed at end of Foundation Stage	Birth to Three Matters	
2004	Every Child Matters: Change for Children. Five outcomes established Choice for Children: the best start for children. A ten year strategy for childcare Children Act: takes forward proposals in Every Child Matters	Effective Provision of Pre-school Education (EPPE) report published	
2005			Children's Workforce Development Council established to support the implementation of ECM with regard to the development of the early years workforce
2006	Childcare Act • Establishes Early Years Foundation Stage Choice for parents. The best start for children. Making it happen. Action plan for the ten year strategy • Free Nursery entitlement (12.5 hours per week) extended from 33 to 38 weeks Plan to extend this to 15 hours for 38 weeks by 2010 and eventually to 20 hrs		Early Years Professional Status standards and prospectus published
2007	The Children's Plan • Ten years vision to improve schools and support children and families		EYPS assessments begin
2008		Early Years Foundation Stage (EYFS) statutory from September 2008 Replaces Curriculum Guidance for the Foundation Stage and Birth to Three Matters	
2010	May 2010. New Coalition government		

2011	Education Act 2011. Government will continue to fund non-statutory early years provision subject to guidance from the Secretary of State for Education	Publication of the Tickell review – The Early Years: Foundations for life, health and learning	EYPS revised. Different pathways, shorter timescales and revised standards
2012		New EYFS framework mandatory from September 2012	CWDC work transferred to the Department for Education. EYPS now overseen by theTDA Revised EYPS standards become statutory Publication of Nutbrown review of early education and childcare qualifications 'Foundations for Quality.' It includes 19 recommendations to improve the skills and knowledge of those who work with young children

Table 2.1 Timeline of influential early years policies and guidelines
Adapted and extended from Early Years Timeline (National Children's Bureau)

Creating policy to support children's development

In the 1990s the incoming Labour government pledged to use research evidence to guide policy and inform changes in early education. They wanted to create an early learning sector based on what was known about effective early learning. This approach, of using evidence to inform what you do, is called evidence-based practice. The government wanted to use research to identify what was the most effective way of supporting young children's development and to use this information to create policies, supported by legislation that enhanced practice and provision.

Using evidence to inform policy

At the outset of this process there was existing evidence about the benefits of early learning. The Head Start programme in the USA had shown that early support and intervention for children and families had positive effects on children's development. This was supported by research which emphasised the importance of early learning on brain development and evidence from developmental psychology which focused on the importance of early diagnosis and intervention for children with learning and developmental needs (Anning and Ball, 2008).

Head Start

Head Start was started in the USA by President Lyndon Johnson in the early 1960s as part of the 'war on poverty'. It continues today as a country-wide comprehensive education, health, nutrition and parent involvement service for children and families with low incomes.

Studies have showed that there were a number of benefits for the children who attended the pre-school programme. All of the studies that collected data on children's cognitive development found that the cognitive development of children who had participated in the programmes was significantly better than children who hadn't attended programmes. One study that looked at 50 other Head Start studies found evidence of immediate improvements, for children attending programmes, in their cognitive and social and emotional development and health.

One of the most influential Head Start programmes was the Highscope/Perry Pre-school programme. This programme was designed for and tracked the lives of 123 African Americans born in poverty and at high risk of failing in school. Participants in this programme have been monitored until the age of 40. It was found that those participants who attended the pre-school programme had higher earnings, were more likely to hold a job, had committed fewer crimes, and were more likely to have graduated from high school than adults who did not attend pre-school.

Taking into account what was already known about the importance of early development, and in response to ongoing concerns and recognised failures in the existing systems, a range of reforms were implemented across services for children and families. This included the establishment of SureStart and the development of the Every Child Matters framework.

SureStart and SureStart local programmes

SureStart emerged from increasing concern about the effects of social exclusion on children's life chances. Evidence shows that between the age of 22 months and 48 months the cognitive and physical development of children from different socio-economic backgrounds begins to drift apart so that by the age of six children from the most deprived backgrounds are often already caught in a cycle of low achievement (Anning and Ball, 2008). SureStart was a radical attempt to change the life chances of these children by supporting their early development.

Definition	
Social exclusion	The process whereby certain groups are pushed to the margins of society and prevented from participating fully by virtue of their poverty, low education or inadequate lifeskills. This distances them from job, income and education opportunities as well as social and community networks. They have little access to power and decision-making bodies and little chance of influencing decisions or policies that affect them, and little chance of bettering their standard of living. **www.cpa.ie/povertyinireland/glossary.htm#S**
Socio-economic group	A way of classifying people that groups them with others of similar social and economic status. The classifications are used by the Office for National Statistics.

The SureStart initiative adopted a holistic approach. Their approach was based on the understanding that the best outcomes for children happen when families, communities and local services for children work together to support children's early growth and development. The aim therefore was to involve all the people around a child to work together to support their early learning and development. The theoretical model that informed this approach was Bronfenbrenner's ecological model of child development (Anning and Ball, 2008). Bronfenbrenner's model shows how children's development is nested within the context of the family, community, settings and services, and wider social and historical influences.

SureStart local programmes were set up in specifically targeted areas of deprivation. They were required to provide a range of services in the home and community to encourage parents to understand and support the development of their children. The programmes were given significant freedoms to design what they would offer. A key feature of the initiative was that local communities were involved in decision making, management and delivery of the services in partnership with other stakeholders such as education, health and social services. This was a new way of working. For the first time providers of services for children were required to work together in partnership, and alongside families and communities, to meet the needs of children and their families. This multi-agency approach was reflected in the 'core services' that the early SureStart programmes had to offer (Anning and Ball, 2008). These included:

Bronfenbrenner's ecological model of child development

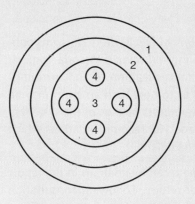

4 Micro-system: for example, the playgroup, pre-school education, childcare or childminder setting where the child actively experiences a particular pattern of events, roles and interpersonal relationships.

3 Meso-system: interrelations between two or more settings in which the child actively participates – for example, home and nursery, childminder and playgroup.

2 Exo-system: settings that do not involve the child as an active participant but in which events occur that affect, or are affected by, what happens in the micro-systems – for example, local authority systems or inspection structures.

1 Macro-system: historical/social/cultural/ecological environments at national policy level.

Figure 2.1 Historical/cultural influences on services for the developing child
(Anning and Ball, 2008)

Bronfenbrenner's model (Figure 2.1) shows how children's development is nested within the context of the family, community, settings and services, and wider social and historical influences.

- outreach and home visiting;

- support for families and parents;

- good-quality play, early learning experiences and childcare;

- healthcare and support for children and their families;

- support for children with additional needs and their families.

It was anticipated that these programmes and services would provide well targeted support and guidance for parents and communities and in doing so enhance the life chances of children. The National Evaluation of SureStart (NESS) assesses the work of SureStart services. The work includes an assessment of how services support developmental outcomes for children. Overall, outcomes have been mixed. Some benefits have been identified but they have often been disappointing in terms of child development. The reasons identified for this apparent lack of progress are quite complex and wide ranging. However, evaluation and research are continuing to try and understand the processes, services and interventions for children and families that best support early development.

ACTIVITY 1

Look at the list of core services provided by SureStart programmes.

- *How do these reflect the aspiration for services for children working together to support children's development?*

- *In what ways do you think services working together will better support children's learning and development?*

Every Child Matters

In 2003 the government published a Green Paper called *Every Child Matters*. This was published in response to a report about the death of a young girl named Victoria Climbié. Lord Laming was appointed to investigate the circumstances leading to and surrounding her death. He was asked to make recommendations as to how such an event may be avoided in the future. The report concluded that there were gross failings of the system in place to protect and safeguard children. The inquiry made 108 recommendations which resulted in fundamental changes to services for children in England.

The Every Child Matters Green Paper aimed to address the recommendations in the report and the government consulted widely on their ideas for reform. Following consultation the necessary legislation was passed in the Children Act in 2004 and the framework *Every child matters: Change for children* was published in November 2004.

The Every Child Matters framework adopted an integrated approach to supporting the development and well-being of children and young people. The framework sets out the aspirations for all children. They are called the five outcomes, which are:

- be healthy;

- stay safe;

- enjoy and achieve;

- make a positive contribution;

- achieve economic well-being.

See Table 2.2.

What the outcomes mean	
Be healthy	Physically healthy Mentally and emotionally healthy Sexually healthy Healthy lifestyles Choose not to take illegal drugs *Parents, carers and families promote healthy choices*
Stay safe	Safe from maltreatment, violence, neglect and sexual exploitation Safe from accidental injury and death Safe from bullying and discrimination Safe from crime and anti-social behaviour in and out of school Have security, stability and are cared for *Parents, carers and families provide safe homes and stability*
Enjoy and Achieve	Ready for school Attend and enjoy school Achieve stretching national educational standards at primary school Achieve personal and social development and enjoy recreation Achieve stretching national educational standards at secondary school *Parents, carers and families support learning*
Make a positive contribution	Engage in decision making and support the community and environment Engage in law abiding and positive behaviour in and out of school Develop positive relationships and choose not to bully and discriminate Develop self confidence and successfully deal with significant live changes and challenges Develop enterprising behaviour *Parents, carers and families promote positive behaviour*
Achieve economic well-being	Engage in further education employment or training on leaving school Ready for employment Live in decent homes and sustainable communities Access to transport and material goods Live in households free from low income *Parents carers and families are supported to be economically active*

Table 2.2 The five outcomes

Every Child Matters: Change for Children DFES (2004) **www.education.gov.uk/ publications/standard/publicationDetail/Page1/DfES/1081/2004**

All organisations that work with children and young people, aged from birth to nineteen, were required to work together to achieve these outcomes for children and their families. This marked a change in the way that provision had been organised. Services for children that had previously worked in different and separate ways now had to develop ways to work together to respond to the needs of children and their families. This included health, education and social services as well as the police and criminal justice system. The way in

27

which early years contributes to children's learning and development is monitored and assessed by OFSTED in their framework for inspection of early years settings.

Following the change of government in 2010 this policy of working together to achieve the best outcomes for children remains an important principle underpinning work with children and families. There are proposed changes to how services are provided and funded, including a greater emphasis on targeted rather than universal provision, but the fundamental aim of supporting the education, health and well-being of children to enable them to reach their potential and make a positive contribution to society remains the cornerstone of provision in early years.

Creating evidence to inform policy

In addition to existing evidence on the impact of early learning on children's development the Labour government commissioned their own research to investigate the effects of pre-school education and explore the characteristics of effective practice. It is called the EPPE study (The Effective Provision of Pre-school Education). The study ran from 1997 to 2003. The study found that attending pre-school had many beneficial effects on children's development, particularly for children who came from disadvantaged backgrounds. The study also found that integrated settings, those that provided education and care, were most effective in supporting development and achieving good outcomes for children. A follow up study published in 2009 found that the quality of pre-school provision can moderate the impact of risks to a child's cognitive development. The outcomes from the study have been very influential in shaping governmental early years policy.

THEORY FOCUS

The Effective Provision of Pre-school Education (EPPE) study

Key findings on the effects of pre-school at age five and also at age seven

- *Impact of attending a pre-school – lasting effects*
  - Pre-school experience, compared to none, enhances all round development in children
  - The duration of attendance is important, with an earlier start being related to better intellectual development
  - Disadvantaged children in particular can benefit significantly from quality pre-school experiences.

- *Does type of pre-school matter?*
  - Taking account of a child's background and prior intellectual skills the type of pre-school a child attends has an important effect on developmental progress. EPPE found that integrated centres (these are centres that fully combine education with care and have a high proportion of trained teachers) and nursery schools (who also have trained teachers) tend to promote the strongest intellectual outcomes for children
  - Similarly fully integrated settings and nursery classes (in school) tend to promote better social development even after taking account of children's backgrounds and prior social development.

- *Effects of quality*
  - Pre-school quality was significantly related to children's scores on standardised tests of reading and maths at age six
  - Settings that have staff with higher qualifications have higher quality scores and their children make more progress.
- *The importance of home learning*
  - the quality of the home learning environment promotes more intellectual and social development than parental occupation or qualification.

Sylva and Pugh (2005)

Creating policy from evidence

The policy of providing services and frameworks to support children's early learning and development is evident in a range of initiatives in early years. These include the development of children's centres, the establishment of the Early Years Professional Status (EYPS), and a range of frameworks to support practice and monitor the quality of provision, including the Early Years Foundation Stage (EYFS) and OFSTED frameworks for inspection.

Children's centres

Children's centre's emerged from the SureStart model of providing targeted local services for children and families. Before the initial planned ten years of SureStart local programmes had come to an end, government policy changed. The new policy was to establish a children's centre in every community. These centres bring together all services for young children and families at one point of contact. This includes pre-school education, health and social care services and training, employment and job advice. This bringing together of services supports the integrated aims of the Every Child Matters outcomes. The centres were initially situated in areas with high indices of deprivation. The aims behind the children's centres are the same as the SureStart local programmes; to provide support and advice to families to enable them to support their child's early development and so offer them a good start in life. It was anticipated that these services would be universal by 2010: all communities would have a children's centre.

Definition	
Indices of deprivation	The Index of Multiple Deprivation combines a number of indicators, chosen to cover a range of economic, social and housing issues, into a single deprivation score for each small area in England. This allows each area to be ranked relative to one another according to their level of deprivation.

The change of government in 2010 marked a change in policy on children's centres. The government have continued to support early years through the work in children's centres but with a different focus. There is no longer an aim for universal provision but for more targeted support in areas judged to have the greatest need. This includes 15 hours a week free entitlement to Nursery education for all two year olds living in disadvantaged communities. The government wants to use payment by results as an incentive for local authorities and children's centres to focus on the core purposes that they have defined.

Definition	
Payment by results	A method of payment in which payment is dependent upon evidence that defined outcomes have been achieved.

These core purposes were developed in response to the Tickell review of early years which reiterated the significance of the early years as a firm foundation for life. These core purposes are reflected in the revised Early Years Foundation Stage (2012) which has a new structure of prime and specific subjects, a fewer number of learning outcomes and a different assessment structure (see below and Chapter 5). The new core purposes of children's centres are defined as follows.

- Child development and school readiness – supporting communication, emotional and physical development so children start school confident and able to learn.

- Parenting aspirations and parenting skills – helping parents to maximise their skills and give their children the best start.

- Child and family health and life chances – promoting good physical and mental health for children and their parents, including addressing risk factors early on.

Children's centres, working in partnership with local authorities are tasked with shaping their services to support these core purposes. The government are also consulting on new ways to run children's centres, such as local cooperatives, so that communities can be more involved in defining and shaping local services.

ACTIVITY **2**

Make sure that you understand the changes in the focus of funded Early Years services in children's centres.

- *What do you think are the benefits of universal provision? What are the benefits of targeted provision? Think about the whole range of issues involved: economic, political, social and moral.*

- *What do you think about the process of payment by results? What are the positives? What are the difficulties?*

- *How may the system of a focus on particular outcomes affect provision and practice in a children's centre?*

- *How may the system of payment by results affect provision and practice in a children's centre?*

ACTIVITY *2* *continued*

- If the system of payment by results is only used in children's centres which are targeted in particular areas what are the implications for children outside these areas? Think about both the advantages and disadvantages.

Early Years Professional Status (EYPS) and the graduate lead

The changing pattern of provision in early years has involved a reconfiguration of the workforce. Children's services require a range of different roles to fulfil the aim of supporting children and families effectively and improving outcomes for children. The Children's Workforce Development Council (CWDC) was responsible, until 2012, for developing the workforce in Early Years to match the requirements in the sector. The early years professional and the graduate lead are part of this workforce development.

The EPPE study concluded that outcomes for children were best in settings led by a graduate. The aim is therefore to create a graduate led early years workforce. Early Childhood Studies degrees are designed to offer the breadth of understanding required to work in children's services and to support the Every Child Matters outcomes.

Early Years Professional Status is a postgraduate qualification. It is competency based, with candidates demonstrating their own understanding of effective early years practice and their ability to lead and manage the practice of others and the setting. There are a number of pathways to achieving EYPS depending on experience and relevance of degree to working in an early years setting within a multi-agency team. The aim was to have a graduate with Early Years Professional Status leading practice in all children's centres by 2010 and in all daycare settings by 2015.

The change of government in 2010 involved a change of emphasis and focus in the early years workforce. Professor Cathy Nutbrown undertook a review of early education and childcare qualifications (2012) which is likely to result in change. Nutbrown (2012, p.10) sets out her vision for the early childhood education and care, namely:

- every child is able to experience high-quality care and education whatever type of home or group setting they attend;

- early years staff have a strong professional identity, take pride in their work, and are recognised and valued by parents, other professionals and society as a whole;

- high-quality early education and care are led by well-qualified early years practitioners;

- the importance of childhood is understood, respected and valued.

In line with this vision, Nutbrown has made a series of recommendations to the government about changes that she regards as necessary to achieve this. It is anticipated that this will result in significant changes in the early years workforce. Proposed changes are set out in the government document 'More Great Childcare' (2013).

ACTIVITY 3

Read through the EPPE research outcomes and the sections on children's centres, Early Years Foundation Stage and Early Years Professional Status.

- *In what ways has the EPPE research influenced early years policy?*

- *How might these initiatives enhance children's early development?*

- *How may positive early development enhance the life chances of children?*

Read the foreword and executive summary of the Nutbrown review, available at **www. education.gov.uk/nutbrownreview**

- *How do her recommendations map to the findings of the EPPE study?*

- *How may her recommendations enhance the development of young children?*

- *What is your view of her recommendations? Give reasons for your view.*

Frameworks for practice

The Early Years Foundation Stage

The Early Years Foundation Stage (EYFS) is the statutory framework for the Foundation Stage. It became a requirement from September 2008 in all OFSTED registered settings. The initial framework replaced the Curriculum Guidance for the Foundation stage, Birth to Three Matters and the National Standards for under 8s Daycare and childminding with a single framework for children from birth to five. The framework set out the legal requirements relating to learning and development and the welfare of children. This framework was replaced in 2012 by a revised framework. The revised framework emerged from the Tickell review which published its findings in 2011: The Early Years: Foundations for life, health and learning. The review made 46 recommendations which included:

- that language and communication, physical and social and emotional development should form the prime areas of learning in the Foundation Stage;

- that there should be a new assessment of a child's learning between 24 and 36 months to identify any emerging difficulties;

- that the existing early learning goals should be reduced and simplified;

- that there should be greater emphasis on working in partnership with parents.

These recommendations were accepted and included in the revised Early Years Foundation Stage (2012).

Learning and development in the EYFS is structured around three prime and four specific areas of learning and safeguarding and welfare standards:

Prime areas:

- personal social and emotional development;

- physical development;

- communication and language.

Specific areas:

- literacy;

- maths;

- understanding the world;

- expressive arts and design.

Safeguarding and welfare standards:

- child protection;

- suitable people;

- key person;

- staff:child ratios;

- health;

- managing behaviour;

- safety and suitability of premises, environment and equipment;

- equal opportunities;

- information and records.

The EYFS provides a framework for practitioners that outlines typical developmental progress towards a series of Early Learning Goals. The framework offers advice on how to provide opportunities to support children's development towards these goals through the development of positive relationships and an enabling environment. Early years practitioners are required to use play as the vehicle for learning in their settings, and to use observation of children for assessing their learning and development. Practitioners are required to complete a progress check in the prime areas for each two-year-old child, and discuss the assessment with parents. They are also required to complete the Early Years Foundation Stage Profile (EYFSP) in the year in which the child is five. This assessment is discussed with parents and a copy given to the year one teacher in school. The overall results for the profile are reported to the local authority who in turn send the data to the relevant government department.

OFSTED

The Office for Standards in Education (OFSTED) is an independent organisation that regulates and inspects services for children and young people, and for adult learners. They publish the outcomes of their inspections as reports that are publically available. All early years settings in the private voluntary and independent sector (PVI sector) and all childminders must register with OFSTED. OFSTED inspect these registered early years settings and make judgements on the quality of the provision. These judgements are published in their reports.

ACTIVITY 4

Look at the revisited Early Years Foundation Stage (2012).

There are now three prime and four specific areas of learning.

- *What do you think about the choices that have been made about which are prime areas and which are specific?*

- *Why do you think that these ones were chosen?*

- *What are the implications for practitioners of this particular emphasis on certain areas in young children's learning?*

Look at the development matters charts. Advice on what adults could do and what adults could provide is outlined under the headings of positive relationships and enabling environments.

- *How could you use this information in a setting?*

- *What are the implications for practice and provision of providing this sort of information? How does it support practice and provision? How may it restrict practice and provision?*

- *What are the implications for professional development of providing such information? How may it inform professional development? How may it restrict professional development?*

C H A P T E R S U M M A R Y

In this chapter we have considered the policy context of early years; how governmental focus on early years has resulted in a wide range of policy, guidance and workforce development initiatives. It is clear that these initiatives have been developed from a commitment to evidence that identifies the best ways in which to support young children and their families. The main initiatives have been identified and explained: SureStart local programmes and children's centres, Every Child Matters, The Early Years Foundation Stage, OFSTED and Early Years Professional Status.

FURTHER READING

Anning, A and Ball, M (2008) *Improving services for young children. From SureStart to children's centres.* London: Sage.

DFE (2012) *Statutory Framework for the Early Years Foundation Stage.* DFE. **https://www.education. gov.uk/publications/standard/publicationDetail/Page1/DFE-00023-2012**

DFE (2013) *More Great Childcare. Raising quality and giving parents more choice.* Available at **www. education.gov.uk/publications/eOrderingDownload/More%20Greet%20Childcare%20v2.pdf**

James, H, Sylva, K, Melhuish, E, Sammons, P, Siraj-Blatchford, I and Taggart, B (2009) The role of pre-school quality in promoting resilience in the cognitive development of young children. *Oxford Review of Education* 35(3): 331–352.

Nutbrown, C (2012) *Foundations for Quality. An independent review of early education and childcare qualifications.* **www.education.gov.uk/nutbrownreview**

Sylva, K and Pugh, G (2005) Transforming the Early Years in England. *Oxford Review of Education* 31 (1): 11–27.

Tickell, C (2011) *The Early Years: Foundations for life, health and learning.* **www.education.gov.uk/ tickellreview**

www.ness.bbk.ac.uk – National evaluation of SureStart

www.ncb.org.uk – National Children's Bureau

http://eppe.ioe.ac.uk – Effective provision of pre-school education

www.highscope.org – Perry pre-school programme

www.ofsted.gov.uk – Office for Standards in Education

Section 2
Children's development

3 Holistic development

This chapter will enable you to:

- understand what we mean by holistic development;
- see how a holistic approach is evident in the systems and structures in early years;
- recognise that children's play is holistic;
- identify the different aspects of children's development that are evident in their play;
- ensure that the language you use to describe children accurately reflects each child's whole self.

Introduction

This chapter will enable you to understand what is meant by holistic development and why this is important in understanding how children grow and learn. Understanding that children's development is holistic is one of the principles underpinning the use of developmental assessments in early years practice. The chapter will also help you to understand how the language we use to talk about children should acknowledge that each aspect of their learning and development is only one part of the totality of who they are.

What is holistic development?

Holistic development means recognising that children's physical, cognitive, linguistic, emotional and social development are interrelated, inseparable and interdependent. All aspects of young children's development occur simultaneously and each area of their development is affected by the others. Children grow and develop through a complex interplay of all aspects of their development. It is a way of understanding the lived reality of young children's learning and development.

The categories that are used to describe children's growth and development, such as cognitive development or, as in the Early Years Foundation Stage, creative development, may be useful for adults to understand and describe what is happening but are false divisions in terms of what actually happens as children grow and learn.

An understanding of holistic development needs to be embedded at all levels in early years to ensure the best outcomes for children: in the systems and structures that support practice, the learning environment and in practitioner's professional knowledge and understanding.

- The systems and structures in early years; education, health and social care, need to work together to support children's all-round development.

- The learning environment needs to be meaningful for the child and offer opportunities for open-ended play and exploration. Curriculum divisions, such as literacy and history, may be useful divisions for adults but have no meaning for young children.

- Early years practitioners need to recognise the interrelatedness of development in what they provide; this needs to be reflected in how they interact and how they observe and assess children's development as they play.

A holistic approach in early years

Systems and structures

To ensure the best outcomes for young children's development the systems and structures in early years need to acknowledge the holistic nature of children's learning and development; that each aspect of development has to be nurtured because each area has an impact on the others. A good example of this is the Every Child Matters outcomes. The outcomes are based on health, education and social care. All aspects of young children's learning and development are regarded as interrelated and interdependent and all agencies and services that work with children are expected to work together to support the integrated outcomes for children:

- be healthy;

- stay safe;

- enjoy and achieve;

- make a positive contribution;

- achieve economic well-being.

Similarly, children's centres services are designed to support all aspects of children's development. They work within a multi-agency framework in which all services aim to work together to support children and families. Children's centres approach can be described as holistic in that the provision recognises the interdependence of health, education and social services in supporting young children's growth and development.

The learning environment

Learning environments in early childhood settings need to reflect the holistic way children learn and grow. Provision needs to support all aspects of development in a fluid and child-centred way. Children need opportunities, activities and experiences that integrate all aspects of their development. A holistic learning environment should include:

- activities and experience that have meaning for the child;

- opportunities for child-initiated, open-ended play and exploration;

- care routines that are an integral part of each day and support children's well-being and independence;

- warm consistent relationships with staff;

- staff who have a good understanding of child development, including the holistic nature of children's learning, and who know how to support this development through their interaction with children.

Children's play: noticing the holistic nature of children's development in their play

Look at the following case study. Notice how the children experience the activity as a complete integrated experience; a holistic experience. Look at the case study analysis. Notice how all aspects of Ria and Joshua's development are evident in this play experience. Notice how this play experience offers evidence towards a range of developmental steps. The developmental statements are taken from the Early Years Foundation Stage (DFE, 2012).

CASE STUDY

Two children are playing together outdoors. In the play area there is a willow tunnel with a den at the end. The den has a crawl hole to get into it. Inside there are rugs on the floor and some soft toys and books left in the den by other children.

Ria, aged four, and Joshua, aged three, run up and down the tunnel laughing. Joshua follows Ria encouraged to do so by Ria shouting 'come on ... up ... down ... up ... down'. After a few times up and down Ria drops to her knees and crawls up and down the tunnel once and then disappears inside the den. Joshua follows.

Ria sits on the carpet for a short time looking around her then she picks up the soft toys and spends some time sitting them in a line making sure that they are all upright. Once they are all sitting in a line she begins talking to them,

> now ... you have to sit still cos I'm reading this story to you

Ria turns to Joshua.

> I'm reading this book ... do you want to listen?

Ria holds the book so the toys can see the pictures and begins to tell the story to the toys. Occasionally she traces her finger from left to right underneath the writing as she speaks

> there were three owls ... they had feathers and leaves and twigs ... their mummy was gone! ... I want my mummy said Bill ... it was dark and they went outside ... but their mummy came ... and they were all happy

Joshua stands and watches and listens attentively for a short time and then disappears from the den for a while re-appearing with a box of pretend food. He comes into the den and announces:

> Snack time

continued

He sits on the floor next to Ria and together they start to give each of the toys a piece of food. When the box is empty Joshua says:

We need some more they haven't gone any

He jumps up, then flops to his knees and crawls out of the den.

When he has gone Ria quietly counts the toys without food. She points at each one as she counts...

...1...2...3...4

Then she begins to count the ones with food.

Joshua returns with a handful of food. He gives the remaining four toys a piece each and leaves the rest on the floor. He sits down next to Ria.

Prime areas

PSED – Demonstrates friendly behaviour, initiating conversations and forming good relationships with peers.

Communication and language – Listens to others one-to-one when conversation interests them – responds to simple instructions – begins to use more complex sentences to link thoughts – uses talk in pretending that objects stand for something else – uses language to imagine and roles and experiences in play situations – uses talk to organise, sequence and clarify thinking.

Physical development – negotiates space successfully – travels with confidence and skill through equipment.

Specific areas

Literacy – describes main story settings, events and principal characters – looks at books independently – holds books the correct way up and turns pages – knows that print carries meaning and, in English, is read from left to right and top to bottom.

Maths – counts up to three or four objects by saying one number name for each item – shows an interest in number problems – uses number names accurately in play.

Understanding the world – in pretend play, imitates everyday actions and events from own background.

Expressive arts and design – engages in imaginative role play based on first-hand experiences – introduces a storyline or narrative into their play – plays alongside children who are engaged in the same theme – plays cooperatively as part of a group to develop and act out a narrative.

(DFE, 2012)

ACTIVITY **1**

Read the case study and development statements.

- *Identify the evidence in the case study for each of the developmental statements. Look at each child separately.*

- *Explain why the children's experience can be described as holistic.*

- *Why is the analysis completed in the Foundation Stage areas of learning? What are the benefits of this? In what ways may it restrict what we observe and comment on?*

- *How can early years practitioners ensure that the children's experience remain holistic whilst also making sure that they are know about each child's development?*

Holistic development and inclusive language

It is important that a holistic approach to young children is reflected in the language that we use to describe children and their development. Language is a powerful tool that is central to the way that we understand the world. The words that we have create our worlds.

ACTIVITY **2**

Words create worlds

Imagine a tree. Think about how you would respond, what you would do, if it was described as:

1 Shelter

2 Fuel

3 Food

4 Recreation

5 A home

6 Building materials

The words we use to describe the function of the tree changes our orientation towards it. It changes what we do and how we behave. In this example it determines whether we nurture it or kill it! This shows that the language we use can change our approach to things and people. This is a fairly straightforward example of words defining our responses, but the same principle applies in more complex human interactions; the words that we use have a profound effect on the ways in which we perceive and respond to people and phenomena. This can happen in both negative and positive ways.

THEORY FOCUS

Words create worlds

Ken Gergen (1999) highlights the importance of the language that we use. He observes that, if language is the central means by which we carry on our lives together – in the past the present and the future – then our ways of talking and writing become areas for consideration. Our future, he argues, is fashioned from mundane exchanges in families, friendships and organisations, in the informal comments, and stories of daily life. The challenge therefore is to step outside of the realities that we have created by the language that we use and ask significant questions – what are the repercussions of different ways of talking, who gains, who is hurt, who is silenced, which traditions are sustained and which are undermined?

Inclusive language

A child's gender, their socio-economic status, their learning needs, their race or their culture is one part of the totality of who they are. If we are to recognise and adopt a holistic view of children and their learning this needs to be reflected in the language we use in how we speak about children and to children. We need to be aware that the ways in which we use language is powerful in shaping children's perceptions of themselves.

CASE STUDY

New shoes

In the Reception class the children are greeted each morning by the staff. Helen arrives one morning and eagerly comes over to the Mrs Parker, who is at the door, and, pointing to her feet, says:

Look … I've got new shoes

Mrs Parker looks at the shoes and responds:

They are lovely shiny shoes Helen; you'll have to look after them so they stay nice and shiny

Helen smiles and goes in to the classroom.

At group time Mrs Parker points out Helen's new shoes to the other children and asks Helen to tell them all all about her new shoes, where she bought them and why she liked those particular shoes. Another child in the group excitedly points to his shoes

I've got new shoes as well

CASE STUDY *continued*

Says Mark, pointing at his feet.

Wow *says Mrs Parker,* another shiny pair of new shoes. I bet they won't stay shiny for very long!

Mark looks carefully at his shoes:

No, they've already got a bit dirty outside today

ACTIVITY 3

Read through the case study and notice the different way in which Mrs Parker responds to Helen and Mark. Think carefully about how the language used subtly implies certain underlying attitudes to Helen and to Mark.

- *What is the underlying attitude to Helen? What does it imply about the role of girls?*
- *What is the underlying attitude to Mark? What does it imply about the role of boys?*
- *How is this difference reflected in the language used?*
- *Look back at the theory focus 'words create worlds.' In what ways does this exchange reflect Gergen's observation that our everyday mundane exchanges fashion our future? What kind of world are these words creating?*
- *What are the implications of this for children's all round growth and development?*

As Gergen (1999) points out, the mundane exchanges that we engage in in our everyday lives create and maintain a particular view of people and society. It is important therefore that we consider the language we use and ensure that it opens up possibilities for children and recognises all that they are in a holistic way. This is particularly important with our most vulnerable children.

Consider these different ways of referring to a child:

Yes I know him, the Down's child

Yes I know him, Daniel, the child with Down's Syndrome

In the first example the emphasis is placed on Daniel having Down's Syndrome because the condition is referred to first. The effect of referring to a child in this way highlights, labels and categorises the child predominantly as the condition. In the second example the emphasis is different. The child is emphasised by using his name and by referring to the fact that he is a child before referring to the syndrome. By using language in this way we emphasise the humanity and complexity of this person; a person who will have many attributes alongside having Down's Syndrome.

ACTIVITY 4

Consider some of the other labels that we use for children who have additional needs.

- *How could you change the way that you refer to these children to ensure that you reflect the whole person?*

- *What impact may this have on the following?*

  - *How you perceive these children.*
  - *How the children perceive themselves.*
  - *How society perceives these children.*

- *How does this use of language reflect a holistic approach to young children?*

- *Some people argue for a completely different approach. They say that it is important to call people with disabilities 'disabled people,' to reflect the fact that society disables some people through its attitudes and provision. Investigate this viewpoint. What is your considered view?*

C H A P T E R   S U M M A R Y

In this chapter we have considered what is meant by holistic development. We have seen how children's development is best supported if the systems and structures in Early Years, the learning environment and early years practitioners adopt a holistic approach. Through the case study we can see how children's play is holistic and how curriculum area divisions are used to describe development in each area. It is important to realise that the divisions are an adult tool for describing development which have no meaning for very young children. The importance of language in building our understandings of the world is explained. Words create worlds. The importance of using inclusive language is demonstrated and you have been asked to consider your own use of language and how that reflects a holistic approach to young children and their development.

FURTHER READING

Baldock, P (2010) *Understanding cultural diversity in the early years.* London: Sage.

Casey, T (2010) *Inclusive play.* London: Sage.

DFE (2012) *Statutory Framework for the Early Years Foundation Stage.* DFE. **https://www.education.gov.uk/publications/standard/publicationDetail/Page1/DFE-00023-2012**

Gergen, K (1999) *An introduction to social constructionism.* London: Sage.

Kahn, T and Young, N (2007) *Embracing equality. Promoting equality and inclusion in the early years.* Pre-school Learning Alliance.

Lindon, J (2006) *Equality in early childhood. Linking theory and practice.* London: Hodder Arnold.

Waddell, M (1992) *Owl babies.* London: Walker Books.

4 Children's development

This chapter enables you to understand:

- the principles that underpin our understanding of children's development;
- what we mean when we refer to physical, cognitive, linguistic or emotional and social development;
- the established patterns and sequences in children's learning and development in the areas of physical, cognitive (intellectual), linguistic, emotional and social development.

Introduction

This chapter outlines the developmental sequences that children go through as they grow and change. The charts identify expected developmental parameters in physical, intellectual, linguistic, emotional and social development. Categorising and describing development within these areas is a way of understanding and managing information about the expected pace, progress and sequences of children's learning and development and, when necessary, to enable focus on an individual area of development where there are concerns. Underpinning these developmental sequences and norms are a set of very important principles that should inform the use of developmental assessment in early years practice.

Principles of child development

Children's development is holistic

All aspects of children's learning and development are interrelated, inseparable and interdependent. Development, in different areas, occurs simultaneously and each area is affected by development in the other areas.

Children's development has multi-determinants

Children learn and develop through a complex interplay of biological and social factors. Children's learning and development occur as a result of who they are and what they experience. The pace and progress of children's development is determined both by genetic imperative and social experiences.

Children's development also occurs within a context of culture of their lives. This context is determined by culture, community and family and it is influenced by the child themselves. A child is part of the context in which they are conceived, born and develop, and, because social processes are dynamic two-way processes the child will necessarily have an impact on the context in which they grow and learn. The context in which children grow and learn has a significant impact on many aspects of their development.

Children's development occurs in a predictable sequence and direction

The sequence of development in all areas of development usually remains predictable regardless of the pace of progress; for example, walking comes before running, single words come before sentences.

There are, of course exceptions to these sequences, and as Bruce and Meggitt (1999) point out, it may be useful to see developmental patterns as similar rather than the same. They suggest that development may be viewed as a web or network of knowledge, skills and aptitudes rather than always a linear progression. This may be particularly important for children who have special educational needs.

Children's development also follows several directional sequences.

From simple to complex – babbling to single words to a combination of words.

From general to specific – showing pleasure through whole-body movement as a baby to smiling and laughing to the use of words or gesture.

From head to toe – physical development starts with control of the head to sitting to crawling to walking.

From inner to outer – from the control of shoulder movement to arms to hands to fingers.

Children's development is cumulative

Children's development begins before birth and continues after they are born. Each stage of development builds on a previous stage; for example, babbling is an important precursor to speech. This means that children need to go through stages of development with sufficient time and experience at each stage to learn, and to consolidate their learning, to ensure that they have a secure basis for the next stage. Therefore, there should be no urge to move children through developmental stages and sequences quickly. Careful consideration, through observation and assessment of learning, needs to be given at each stage of development to ensure that children have had sufficient time and experience to learn and consolidate their learning before moving on to the next stage of development. Within a free play environment this will happen quite naturally for many children across different areas of learning. As children engage with the activities and experiences the development of their learning will be determined by this interaction. As the need and desire to know and do more motivates children they will determine when and how their learning develops. A well-planned, rich and stimulating learning environment will provide these opportunities for children.

Children's development is characterised by individual variation

Within any group of children there will be a variation in the pace of individual progress within and between developmental areas, and, there will be variation in comparative progress between children. There tends to be greater variation in the development of psychological skills than physical skills and variation increases as children get older (Empson and Nabuzoka, 2004). This is to be expected because children's development has multi-determinants. Developmental charts therefore need to be understood in terms of ranges of age and developmental norms rather than fixed ages linked to stages. It is when children fall significantly outside of these developmental parameters, or there is a significant discrepancy between areas of development, that there should be concern.

Areas of development

These principles of child development understand children's development as holistic, individual and multi-dimensional; it is a complex patterning of interdependent factors. However, for ease of understanding and articulating developmental patterns children's development can be divided into areas.

Developmental patterns are observable in areas of development such as:

- physical development;

- cognitive (or intellectual) development;

- linguistic development;

- emotional development;

- social development.

Using developmental charts in these different areas can be very useful in describing and understanding children's growth and development. It enables parents and practitioners to provide experiences that are sensitive to the child's needs because they are developmentally appropriate. Tracking children's development through the use of charts and sequences enables assessment of children's progress, and, when appropriate, enables assessments to be made about children about whom professionals have concerns.

However, it is also important to be aware that as well as recognising that developmental charts are useful in a number of ways, there is also a risk of using them in ways that restrict understandings, provision and interaction. If, in early years, developmental charts are used as rigid checklists there is a risk that practitioner's understanding of children's development will rely too heavily on external expectations rather than seeing individuals growing and learning within a particular context; they will lose the holistic view of children, childhood and learning. It is a careful balancing act; having the professional knowledge and skill to know what developmental expectations are and using this information to inform assessment, interaction and provision whilst also acknowledging children's individuality.

Development matters in the Early Years Foundation Stage

The patterns of development in these development charts are translated into statements in the Early Years Foundation Stage. The statements in the EYFS outline observable behaviours that demonstrate that a child has reached a particular level of development. For example, between 8 and 20 months the EYFS states that you may observe a child enjoying babbling and increasingly experimenting with using sounds and words to communicate for a variety of purposes. This statement reflects typical development in this age range listed in development charts.

There is a duty on practitioners in settings to observe and assess children's learning against the statements and learning goals in the EYFS. However, developmental charts can also be used alongside the EYFS statements to add detail to assessments and so more fully understand children's learning and development.

Physical development

Introduction

Physical development describes the progress of children's control over their body. Progress is characterised by an increase in skill and complexity of performance. The process of muscular movement is called motor development. Motor movement is divided into gross motor skills and fine motor skills.

Definitions	
Gross motor skill	Whole body movements. Rolling, sitting crawling, standing, walking, running, skipping, jumping, etc. They all require strength, stamina and suppleness to increase co-ordination balance and judgement.
Fine motor skill	The use of hands in co-ordination with the eyes to perform precise finger and hand movement.

The direction of development

Children's physical development follows a particular sequence. See Figure 4.1.

- From head to toe (cephalo-caudal). Head and neck control is acquired initially then control of the spinal muscles then rolling, shuffling and crawling before walking

- From inner to outer (proximo-distal). Brain, spinal column before shoulders, arms, hands, and lastly fine motor control of fingers.

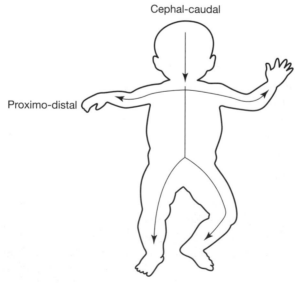

Figure 4.1 Direction of development in children

Physical development charts

The neonate (newborn)

The neonate (newborn)			
Gross motor development	**Fine motor development**	**Vision**	**Reflexes**
Prone (*lying face down*) The baby lies with her head turned to one side resting on the cheek Her body is in a frog-like posture with her bottom up and her knees curled under her tummy Her arms are bent at the elbows and tucked under her chest with fists clenched Supine (*Lying on her back*) The baby lies with head to one side Her knees are bent towards the body with the soles of her feet touching Her arms are bent inwards towards her body Jerky, asymmetric kicking movements can be seen Ventral Suspension (*when the baby is held in the air face down*) The head and legs fall below the level of the back Sitting When the baby is pulled up into a sitting position there is complete head lag. The head falls backwards as the body comes up and then flops forward onto the chest If the baby is held in a sitting position, her back is completely curved and her head is on the chest	The fists are clenched The baby can focus 15–25cm and stares at brightly coloured objects within visual range She concentrates on the carer's face when feeding	Neonates can focus on faces close to their own Research shows that they show preference for the human face They can imitate and may try to copy facial expressions and movements, like sticking your tongue out, but these are not voluntary movements yet Eye contact with parents and carers helps to establish interaction Babies respond to contrasting colours and three-dimensional objects, such as mobiles and baby gyms	A reflex is an automatic involuntary movement made in response to a particular stimulus Babies have a range of survival reflexes called *primitive* reflexes Testing the reflexes of babies helps to assess the health of the central nervous system This should be done by a trained doctor, or other health professional Primitive reflexes *Rooting reflex* – Stimulus: brushing the cheek with a finger or nipple – Response: the baby turns to face the stimulus *Sucking reflex* – Stimulus: placing nipple or teat in the mouth – Response: the baby sucks *Grasping reflex* – Stimulus: placing object in baby's palm – Response: the fingers close tightly round the object *Placing reflex* – Stimulus: brushing top of foot against table top – Response: the baby lifts it's foot and places it on the hard surface *Walking reflex* – Stimulus: held standing feet touching a hard surface – Response: the baby moves her legs forward alternately and walks. *Moro (startle) reflex* – Stimulus: insecure handling or sudden loud noise – Response: the baby throws her head back and the fingers fan out; the arms then return to the embrace posture and the baby cries

Table 4.1 Physical development: The neonate

Physical development. One month to seven years

	Gross motor skills	Fine motor skills
1 month	*Prone (lying face down)* The baby lies with his head to one side but can now lift his head to change position. The legs are bent, no longer tucked under the body *Supine (lying on the back)* The head is on one side. The arm and leg on the side that the head is facing will stretch out *Sitting* The back is a complete curve when the baby is held in sitting position	The baby gazes attentively at carer's face whilst being fed, spoken to or during any caring routines The baby grasps a finger or other object placed in the hand The hands are usually closed
3 months	The baby can now lift up the head and chest supported on elbows, forearms and hands The baby usually lies with the head in a central position. There are smooth, continuous movements of the arms and legs. The baby waves the arms symmetrically and brings hands together over the body There should be little or no head lag. When held in a sitting position the back should be straight, except for a curve in the base of the spine The baby will sag at the knee when held in a standing position. The placing and walking reflexes should have disappeared	Finger play – the baby has discovered its hands and moves them around in the front of the face, watching the movements and the pattern they make in the light The baby holds the rattle or similar object for a short time if placed in the hand. Frequently hits his/herself in the face before dropping it The baby is now very alert and aware of what is going on around The baby moves her head to look around and follows adult movements
6 months	Lifts the head and chest well clear of the floor by supporting on outstretched arms. The hands are flat on the floor. The baby can roll over from front to back The baby will lift her head to look at her feet. She may lift her arms, requesting to be lifted. She may roll over from back to front If pulled to sit, the baby can now grab the adult's hands and pull herself into a sitting position; the head is now fully controlled with the strong neck and muscles. She can sit for long periods with support. The back is straight Held standing she will enjoy weight bearing and bouncing up and down	Bright and alert, looking around constantly to absorb all the visual information on offer Fascinated with small toys within reaching distance, grabbing them with the whole hand, using a palmar grasp Transfers toys from hand to hand Things are often explored by putting them in her mouth

9 months	The baby may be able to support his body on knees and outstretched arms. He may rock backwards and forwards and try to crawl The baby rolls from back to front and may crawl away The baby is now a secure and stable sitter – he may sit unsupported for 15 minutes or more The baby can pull himself to a standing position. When supported by an adult he will step forward on alternate feet He supports his body in the standing position by holding on to a firm object. He may begin to side-step around furniture	Uses the inferior pincer grasp with index finger and thumb Looks for fallen objects out of sight – he is now beginning to realise that they have not disappeared for ever Grasps objects usually with one hand, inspects with the eyes and transfers to the other hand May hold one object in each hand and bang them together Uses the index finger to poke and point Can clasp hands and may imitate others' actions
12 months	Can sit alone indefinitely. Can get into a position from lying down Pulls herself to stand and walks around the furniture Returns to sitting without falling. May stand alone for a short period	Looks for objects hidden and out of sight Uses a mature pincer grasp and releases objects Throws toys deliberately and watches them fall Likes to look at picture books and points at familiar objects Pincer grasp is used; the thumb and first two fingers
15 months	Walks alone, feet wide apart Sits from standing Crawls upstairs	Points at pictures and familiar objects Builds a tower with two bricks Enjoys books; turns several pages at once
18 months	Walks confidently and is able to stop without falling Can kneel, squat, climb and carry things around Tries to kick a ball Walks upstairs with hand held	Uses delicate pincer grasp Scribbles on paper Builds a tower with three bricks
2 years	Runs safely Walks up and downstairs holding on – usually two feet on each step Rides a trike, pushing it along with the feet	Holds a pencil and attempts to draw circles, lines and dots Uses fine pincer grasp with both hands to do complicated tasks Builds a tower of six bricks Can turn the pages of a book singly
3 years	Can stand, walk and run on tiptoe Can walk backwards and sideways Has good spatial awareness Walks upstairs, one foot on each step Rides a tricycle and uses the pedals	Can thread large wooden beads onto a lace Controls a pencil in the preferred hand Can use scissors to cut paper Can copy straightforward shapes such as a circle Builds a tower of nine bricks
4 years	A sense of balance is developing Climbs play equipment Walks up and downstairs, one foot on each step Can stand, walk and run on tiptoe Can catch, throw, bounce and kick a ball	Builds a tall tower of bricks Can build other constructions also Grasps a pencil maturely Beginning to do up buttons and fasten zips Can thread small beads on a lace

continued

	Gross motor skills	Fine motor skills
5 years	Can hop Can use a variety of play equipment – swings, climbing frames, slides Plays ball games well Can walk along on balancing beam	Can draw a person with head, trunk, legs and eyes, nose and mouth Can sew large stitches Good control of pencils and paintbrushes
6 years	Has increased agility, muscle coordination and balance across all activities Rides a two-wheeled bicycle Kicks a football well Makes running jumps	Can catch a ball with one hand Writing hold is similar to the adult Can draw a person in increasing detail, for example, with hair style and eyebrows
7 years	Can climb and balance well on the apparatus Hops easily on either foot, keeping well balanced	Writes well Can sew neatly with a large needle

Table 4.2 Physical development: one month to seven years

Cognitive development

Introduction

Cognitive development is concerned with the construction of thought processes. It is concerned with how we acquire, organise and use what we learn. It involves the development of conceptual and conscious thought, memory, problem solving, imagination and creativity.

Cognitive development chart. Birth to seven years

Age	Cognitive development
Birth	Are able to explore using the senses Are beginning to develop basic concepts such as hunger, cold, wet
1 month	Will begin to recognise main carer and respond with movement, cooing Will repeat pleasurable movements, thumb-sucking, wriggling
3–4 months	Are more interested in their surroundings Begin to show an interest in playthings Begin to understand cause and effect – if you move a rattle, it will make a sound
5–6 months	Expect things to behave in certain ways – the jack-in-the-box will pop up, but is unlikely to play a tune Will reach for things with growing co-ordination Will recognise familiar everyday things – e.g. cot, changing mat
9 months	Recognises pictures of familiar things Watches a toy being hidden and then looks for it (object permanence established) Memory develops – children can remember, anticipate and respond to regular daily patterns, e.g. feeding and sleeping routines, waving

12–15 Months	Explore objects using trial-and-error methods Begin to point and follow when others point Begin to treat objects in appropriate ways-cuddle a doll, talk into a telephone Seeks out hidden objects
18 months–2 years	Refer to themselves by name Begin to understand the consequences of their own actions; for example, pouring the juice makes a wet patch Develop the ability to symbolise – use one thing to represent another
3 years	Can match primary colours Can sort objects into categories, but usually by only one criterion at a time; for example, all the cars from a selection of vehicles, but not the cars that are red Further develop their capacity to symbolise through the use of language (anticipating later literacy skills of reading and writing)
4 years	Can sort with more categories Can solve simple problems, usually by trial and error, but begin to understand 'why' Adding to their knowledge by continually asking questions Memory skills developing, particularly around significant events (such as holidays and birthdays), and familiar songs and stories Include representative detail in drawings, often based on observation Will confuse fantasy and reality – 'I had a tiger come to tea at my house too' Understand that writing carries meaning and use writing in play Social and cultural conventions increasingly influence their drawing and writing
5 years	Has a good sense of past, present and future Are becoming literate – most will recognise own name and write it, respond to books and are interested in reading Demonstrate good observational skills in their drawings Understand the one-to-one principle and can count reliably to 10 Concentration is developing – can concentrate without being distracted for about 10 minutes at an appropriate task Thinking becomes increasingly co-ordinated and children become able to hold more than one point of view in mind
6 years	Begin to understand the mathematical concept of measuring – time, weight, length, capacity, volume Are interested in why things happen and hypothesis; for example, that seeds need water to grow Begin to use symbols in their drawing and painting – the radial sun and the strip sky appear now Many children will begin to read independently, but there is a wide individual variation in this Can concentrate for longer periods of time
7 years	Are able to conserve number reliably; that is, recognise that a number of objects remains constant however they are presented May be able to conserve mass and capacity Begin to deal with number abstractly; can perform calculations involving simple addition and subtraction mentally May be able to tell the time from a watch or clock Are developing an ability to reason and an understanding of cause and effect

Table 4.3 Cognitive development: birth to seven years

Children's cognitive development needs to be supported by adults through interaction and the provision of appropriate activities and experiences.

- *Choose an age range and suggest a range of appropriate activities and experiences to support children's cognitive development.*

- *Look at the next stage of development from the one you have chosen. How could you extend and adapt the activities and experiences that you have identified to encourage the next stage of development?*

Remember that daily routines such as shopping or sorting washing provide excellent opportunities for supporting children's learning and development.

Language development

Introduction

Language is the main way in which we think and communicate. We are the only species that has the ability to use language. Other species communicate, but in ways that specifically meet their needs; for example, by making their fur stand on end to communicate danger, by spraying their territory to mark it out, or growling to deter attackers. They are not able to think only to respond instinctively.

We live in a complex world that requires a sophisticated process to enable us to think and to communicate. Language is that process. Language is learned through social interaction within the society in which we each grow and learn.

Children's language develops through a series of identifiable sequential stages The pace of children's progress depends partly upon their chronological age, i.e. maturational development of sound-producing physiology, but it is also profoundly influenced by their experience of language in the home, community and setting in which they grow and learn. It is important to take into account the impact of these factors when assessing children's developmental progress.

Language development chart

Language development. Birth to five years

Approximate age	Developmental level
Birth	• Involuntary cry
2–3 weeks	• Signs of intentional communication: eye contact
6 weeks onward	• Children may smile when spoken to • Cooing and gurgling begin in response to parent or carer's presence and voice, also to show contentment

1–2 months	• Children may move their eyes or head towards the direction of the sound • Children begin to discriminate between consonant sounds
3 months	• Children will raise their head when sounds attract their attention
4–5 months	• Playful sounds appear, most are in response to the human voice and to show contentment • Cooing and laughing appear • Children respond to familiar sounds by turning their head, kicking or stopping crying • Shout to attract attention
6 months	• The beginning of babbling regular repeated sounds and playing around with these sounds. This is important for practising sound-producing mechanisms necessary for later speech • Babbling is 'reduplicated babbling' at this stage – consonants (C) and vowels (V) together in repeated CV syllables ba ba ba ba ba • Coooing, laughing and gurgling become stronger • Children begin to understand emotion in the parent or carer's voice • Children begin to enjoy music and rhymes, particularly if accompanied by actions
9 months	• Babbling continues and the repertoire increases • Babbling is now 'variegated' – children produce strings of different sounds ba-ma • Babbling takes on the stresses and intonation of the language (or languages) that they are hearing • Children begin to recognise their own name • The range of vowel sounds produced start to resemble the language that the child is hearing – they are 'tuning' in to the language around them • May understand simple, single words like 'No' or 'Bye-Bye' • Children continue to enjoy music and rhymes and will now attempt to join in with the actions e.g. Pat-a-cake
9–12 months	• Babbling reflects the intonation of speech • Consonants begin to reflect the language that they are hearing • Children may imitate simple words. This is usually an extension of babbling e.g. dada • Pointing begins. This is often accompanied by a sound or the beginnings of a word. This demonstrates an increasing awareness that words are associated with people and objects
12 months	• Children's vocabulary starts to develop but often remains quite limited as children concentrate on achieving mobility • Passive vocabulary increases rapidly • Pointing accompanied by a single word is the basis of communication
15 months	• Children's active vocabulary increases: this tends to be names of familiar things and people • Children use their language to name belongings and point out named objects • Children over extend words, e.g. 'Dog' for all furry animals with four legs • Less frequently they under extend words e.g. 'Cat' only for their cat not the one next door • One word and intonation is used to indicate meaning e.g. 'Cup' may mean 'I want a drink'/'I have lost my cup', etc. The intonations and possibly the situation would indicate the meaning to people who are familiar with the child. This is called the holophrasic stage • Children will repeat words or sentences
21 months	• Both passive and active vocabularies rapidly increase; the passive vocabulary however, remains larger than the active • Children begin to name objects and people that are not there; this shows the development of language for thinking • Sentences begin. Initially as two-word phrases, e.g. 'Mummy gone' • Gesture is still a fundamental part of communication • Children begin asking questions usually, 'What?', 'Who?', etc.

continued

Approximate age	Developmental level
2 years	• Both active and passive vocabularies continue to increase • Children can generalise words but this sometimes means they over generalise e.g. all men are 'daddy' • Personal pronouns (words instead of actual names) are used e.g. he she etc. They are not always used correctly • Sentences become longer although they tend to be in telegraphic speech i.e. only the main sense-conveying words are used like 'Mummy gone work' • Questions are asked frequently, 'What?' 'Why?' • The plural form of words is often over generalised, children may refer to mouses or sheeps • Irregular verb forms may be used, i.e. seed (for saw) and comed (for came) • In speech final consonants and unstressed syllables often omitted i.e. 'ca' for 'cat' and 'gin' for 'begin' • Consonant sounds that are similar to the ear are often confused, t/k/p d/g/b b/v
2 years 6 months	• Vocabulary increases rapidly; there is less imbalance between passive and active vocabularies • Word use is more specific so there are fewer over- and under- generalisations • Sentences get longer and more precise, although they are still usually abbreviated versions of adult sentences • Word order in sentences is sometimes incorrect • Children can use language to protect their rights and interests and to maintain their own comfort and pleasure, e.g. 'It's mine', 'Get off' • Children can listen to stories and are interested in them
3 years	• Vocabulary develops rapidly; new words are picked up quickly • Sentences continue to become longer and longer and more like adult speech • Children talk to themselves whilst playing to plan and order their play which is evidence of children using language to think • Stylistic variation (speaking differently in different contexts) is usually well developed • Language can now be used to report on what is happening, direct their own and others' actions, to express ideas and to initiate and maintain friendships • Antonyms are often confused (early/late, today/yesterday) as children begin to engage with the meaning of more abstract words • Pronouns are usually used correctly • Questions are used frequently • Rhymes and melody are attractive to children
4 years	• Children's vocabulary is now extensive; new words are added regularly • Longer and more complex sentences are used; sentences may be joined with because, which demonstrates an awareness of causes and relationships • Children are able to narrate long stories, including the sequence of events • Play involves running commentaries • The boundaries between fact and fiction are blurred and this is reflected in speech • Speech is fully intelligible with few, minor incorrect uses • Questioning is at its peak • Children can usually use language to: share, take turns, collaborate, argue, predict what may happen, compare possible alternatives, anticipate, give explanations, justify behaviour, create situations in imaginative play, reflect upon their own feelings and begin to describe how other people feel

5 years	• Children have a wide range of vocabulary and can use it appropriately
	• Vocabulary can include colours, shapes, numbers and common opposites
	• Sentences are usually correctly structured, although incorrect grammar may still be used
	• Pronunciation may still be childish
	• Language continues to be used and developed, as described in the section on 4 year olds: this may now include phrases heard on the television and associated with children's toys
	• Questions and discussions are for enquiry and information; questions become more precise as children's cognitive skills develop
	• Children will offer opinions in discussion
	• Children are still learning to understand ambiguities and subtleties in language, e.g. irony and metaphor

Table 4.4 Language development: birth to five years

ACTIVITY 2

Look back through the chart on children's language development.

- *Outline the development of children's use of questioning in their language development*

- *Suggest why questioning develops and changes in this way between the ages of 21 months and five years*

  - *think about children's overall proficiency in language and their cognitive capabilities – how does their questioning reflect this development?*

Language development. Five to seven years

Joan Tough's seven uses of language

Between the ages of five and seven years children use, practise, adapt and refine their language knowledge and skills. Children now use language for a wide range of purposes. Joan Tough (1976) identifies seven different uses of language. They provide a useful way of understanding and describing the ways in which children use language. Tough (1976) argues that the uses of language are hierarchical; children progress through the seven uses in the stated order. The early stages will be observed in most children's language by the age of five years (Table 4.5).

Use	Using language to
1. Self-maintaining	1.1 Protect oneself: Stop it Go Away You're hurting me 1.2 Meet psychological and physical needs: I'm thirsty You're hurting me
2. Directing	2.1 Directing actions of self and others: You push the lorry round the track I just need to put this brick here then I've finished

continued

Use	Using language to
3. Reporting	3.1 Label the component parts of a scene: There is a car, a lorry and a bus 3.2 Refer to detail, the colour and the shape, size or position of an object 3.3 Talk about an incident 3.4 Refer to a sequence of events: We walked to the bus stop and then caught the bus to school 3.5 Reflect on the meanings of experiences, including feelings: I like playing in the shop, especially with Sarah
4. Towards logical reasoning	4.1 Explain a process 4.2 Recognise causal and dependent relationships: You have to put sugar in this tea or it's not very nice 4.3 Recognise problems and their causes 4.4 Justify judgements and actions: I didn't want to go out because I hadn't finished my drawing
5. Predicting	5.1 Anticipate or forecast: We're going to have a hamster and a cage with a wheel 5.2 Predict the consequences of actions or events: That propeller will fall off if you don't stick it on properly
6. Projecting	6.1 Project into the experiences, feelings and reactions of others: He was stuck in there and couldn't get out and was frightened. 6.2 Project into a situation never experienced: I wouldn't like to be a rabbit and live in a cage, would you?
7. Imagining	7.1 In an imagined context: Hello, this is Hot Scissors hairdressers. Would you like to make an appointment?

Table 4.5 The seven uses of language (five to seven years)

Consonant acquisition

Between the ages of 18 months and six years children gradually acquire, use, practise and refine their use of consonants. There is a pattern and developmental sequence to the acquisition of consonants.

Definitions	
Consonant	• In common usage it refers to the letter of the alphabet that denotes a consonant sound. In English these are b c d f g h j k l m n p q r s t v w x z and in some instances y (for example in yoke) • Consonants are produced with the lips (p), front of the tongue (t), back of the throat (k), in the throat (h), and with air through the nose (m, n) • More precisely, in linguistics, it is recognised that there are more consonant sounds than letters. For example, in English we have consonant sounds of 'th' 'sh' 'ch' and 'zh'. The International Phonetic Alphabet (IPA) uses a unique symbol to represent each consonant
Vowel	• The sounds a e i o u and, in English, in some instances y. For example in the word 'myth' the y denotes the vowel sound i • Vowels are produced with an open vocal tract

Average age of consonant acquisition	
18 months	p b m h n w
2 years	k g d t 'ng'
2.5 years	f y
3 years	r l s
3.5 years	'ch' 'sh'
4 years	z j
4.5 years	'th' (as in thin)
5 years	'th' (as in the)
6 years	'zh' as in trea*su*re

Table 4.6 Consonant acquisition

Emotional and social development

Introduction

Emotional development is the growth of a child's ability to feel and express an increasing range of emotions appropriately. It includes the development of emotional responses to oneself, to other people and to what we say and do. Development is the progression towards the capability to feel and express emotions in ways that contribute to our own and others' well-being.

Social development is the growth of a child's ability to relate to others appropriately within the social context of their life. It includes the development of social skills and skills of independence. As children learn and develop social skills this has an impact on their ability to engage in social play alongside and with other children in a group. Social play also follows a developmental pattern. This pattern is described in this chapter but is not aligned with an age as the development of social play depends very strongly upon a child's opportunities to play with other children.

An important strand in emotional and social development is the development of self-concept and self-image. This is the view we have of ourselves and our beliefs about how other people see us.

Within the context of their emotional and social development children also learn expected patterns of behaviour. The development of children's understanding of these expectations and their ability to manage and control themselves in accordance with these expectations are closely linked to their emotional and social development. This chapter outlines typical developmental aspects of children's behaviour as they become aware of and engage with society's expectations.

Children's development in each of these areas is detailed in a chart below. You will notice that the charts detail similar developmental patterns. This is to be expected as children's behaviour, their development of self-image and their social play are very closely linked to their emotional and social development.

General principles of emotional and social development

There are important understandings about the context of children's development that must be taken into consideration when studying or assessing children's emotional and social development.

- Development is a holistic process; all areas of development are interdependent. This is particularly evident in the development of emotional and social skills which, when disordered, can have a profound impact on other areas of development.

- Development often occurs in periods of rapid growth followed by a period of relative stability. During the period of stability children consolidate what they have learned.

- The path of development moves from complete immaturity and dependence towards emotional and social maturity and independence.

- Children develop emotionally and socially within a context. Children grow and learn within family systems. Families exist within a larger social and cultural context. Both family and cultural context have a profound effect upon children's emotional and social development, including their behaviour and their sense of self.

Emotional and social development chart. Birth to seven years

Age	Emotional and social development
Birth At this age babies…	• Are utterly dependent on others. • Have rooting, sucking and swallowing reflexes. • Sleep most of the time. • Prefer to be left undisturbed. • Startle to noise, and turn to the light, providing it is not bright. • Cry when hungry, in pain, or unattended to. • Are usually content in close contact with carer. • Are not aware of themselves as separate beings.
1 month Around this age babies…	• Sleep most of the time when not being handled or fed. • Cry for their needs to be attended to (different cry for different need). • Will turn to the breast. • Look briefly at a human face. • Will quieten in response to human voice and smile in response to the main carer's voice. • Develop a social smile and respond with vocalisation to the sight and sound of a person (at around 6 weeks); the baby's response to a person separate from themselves. • Grasp a finger if the baby's hand is open and palm is touched. • Gradually learn to recognise themselves as separate individuals.

2 months Around this age babies usually…	• Stop crying when they are picked up. • Sleep less during the day and more during the night. • Explore, using their five different senses. • Differentiate between objects, and begin to tell one face from another. • Follow a human face when it moves. • Smile and become more responsive to others.
3 months Around this age infants usually…	• Respond to friendly handling and smile at most people. • Use sounds to interact socially and reach out to the human face. • Become more orientated to their mothers and other main carer's, and look at their carers face when feeding. • Begin to connect what they hear with what they see. • Are able to show an increasingly wide range of feelings and responses. • Have some awareness of the feelings and emotions of others. • Still react to the world as if they alone make things exist or disappear.
6 months Around this age infants…	• Become more aware of themselves in relation to other people and things. • Show a marked preference for their main carer(s). • Reach out for familiar people and show a desire to be picked up and held. • Begin to be more reserved with, or afraid of, strangers. • Smile at their own imagine in the mirror. • May like to play hide and seek or peek-a-boo. • Show eagerness, anger and pleasure by body movement, facial expression, and vocally. • Play alone with contentment. • Stop crying when communicated with.
9 months Around this age infants usually…	• Clearly distinguish familiar people and show a marked preference for them. • Show a fear of strangers and need reassurance when in their company, often clinging to the main adult and hiding their face in them. • Play peek-a-boo, copy hand clapping and pat a mirror image. • Still cry for attention to their needs, but also use their voice to attract people to themselves. • Show some signs of willingness to wait for attention. • Show pleasure and interest at familiar words. Understand 'No'. • Try to copy sounds. • Offer objects to others but do not release them.
12 months Around this age infants usually…	• Enjoy looking at themselves and things around them in a mirror. • Know their name and respond to it. • Like to be within sight and hearing of a familiar adult. • Can distinguish between different members of the family and act socially with them. • Will wave goodbye. • Appreciate an audience, repeating something that produced a laugh before. • Begin to imitate actions they have seen others do. • Respond affectionately to certain people. • May be shy with strangers. • Are capable of a variety of emotional responses. • Show rage when thwarted. • Actively seek attention by vocalising rather than by crying. • Will obey simple instructions. • Recognise other people's emotions and moods and express their own. • Learn to show love to others, if they have been shown love themselves.

continued

Age	Emotional and social development
15 months Around this age children…	• Use their main carer as a safe base from which to explore the world and are anxious and apprehensive about being physically separated from carers. • Are very curious about their environment and their exploration can lead to conflict with their carers. • Have a sense of 'me; and 'mine', begin to express themselves defiantly. • Begin to distinguish between 'you' and 'me'. • Can point to members of the family in answer to questions. • Tend to show off. • Are not dissuaded from undesirable behaviour by verbal reasoning and react poorly to the sound of sharp discipline (the best way to manage behaviour at this stage is to distract the child and change the environment) • Have an interest in strangers but may be fearful and wary of them. • Show jealousy of the attention of adults that is given to other children. • Throw toys when angry. • Are emotionally changeable. • Resist change in routines or sudden transitions. • Swing from dependence to wanting to be independent. • May hold a cup and drink without assistance, hold a spoon and bring it to the mouth, help with dressing and undressing.
18 months At this age children usually…	• Tend to follow their carers around, be sociable and imitate them by helping with small household tasks. • Respond by stopping doing something when the word 'no' is used but this usually needs reinforcement. • Imitate and mimic others during their play. • Engage in solitary or parallel play but like to do this near a familiar adult or sibling. • Show some social emotions, for example, sympathy for someone who is hurt. • Cannot tolerate frustration. • Show intense curiosity. • Have intense mood swings, from dependence to independence, eagerness to irritation, and co-operation to resistance. • Try to establish themselves as members of the social group. • Begin to internalise the values of the people around them. • Are conscious of their family group. • Are still very dependent on familiar carers and often return to a fear of strangers. • Can use a cup and spoon well, and successfully get food into their mouth. • Take off some clothing and help with dressing themselves. • Although still in nappies can make their carers aware of their toileting needs – through words or restless behaviour.
2 years Around this age children…	• Can be sensitive to the feelings of others. • Display emotions such as sympathy. • Are capable of being loving and responsive. • Demand their carer's attention and want their needs to be met immediately. • Sometimes have tantrums if crossed or frustrated or if they have to wait for attention or for the satisfaction of their needs. • They will ask for food. • Can sometimes respond to being asked to wait. Are possessive of their own toys and objects, have little idea of sharing. • Tend to be easily distracted by an adult if they are frustrated or angry. • Join in when an adult sings or tells a simple story. Can point to parts of the body and other things when asked. • Are sometimes self-contained and independent, other times very dependent.

2 years 6 months Around this age children…	• Develop their sense of self-identity; they know their name, their position in the family and their gender. • Play with other children – this begins to reinforce their gender role – they learn that different toys may be intended for girls and boys. • Engage in 'pretend' play including make-believe and role play. • Behave impulsively, wanting to have anything that they see, and do anything that occurs to them. • Throw tantrums when thwarted and are less easily distracted. • Are often in conflict with their carers. • May be aware of and avoid certain hazards like hot ovens and stairs. • Able to use a spoon well. • Able to pour from one container to another therefore able to get themselves a drink. • Dress with supervision – unzip zips, buckle and unbuckle, button up and undo buttons. • Are toilet trained during the day and may be at night especially if lifted (taken to the toilet during the night).
3 years Around this age children…	• Can feel secure when in a strange place away from their carers, as long as they are with people with whom they became familiar when their carer was present. • Can wait for their needs to be met. • Are less rebellious and use language rather than physical outbursts to express themselves. • Still respond to distraction as a method of controlling their behaviour, but are ready to respond to reasoning and bargaining. • Are beginning to learn the appropriate behaviour for a range of different social settings – for example, they are aware when they need to be quiet and when they can be noisy. • Adopt the attitudes and moods of adults. • Want the approval of loved adults. • Can show affection for younger siblings. • Can share things and take turns. • Enjoy make-believe play. • Use dolls and toys to act out their experiences. May have imaginary fears and anxieties. • Towards the end of this year may show some insecurity expressed as shyness, irritability and self-consciousness. • May have the ability to use implements to eat with. • Toilet themselves during the day, may be dry at night. • Will wash their hands but may have difficulty drying them. • Are learning to dress without supervision.
4 years By this age children…	• Can be very sociable and talkative to adults and children, enjoy 'silly' talk. • May have one particular friend. • Can be confident and self-assured. • May be afraid of the dark and have other fears. Have taken the standards of behaviour of the adults to whom they are closest. • Turn to adults for comfort when overtired, ill or hurt. • Play with groups of children – groups tend to centre round an activity, them disperse and reform. • Can take turns but not consistently. • Are often very dramatic in their play – engage in elaborate and prolonged imaginative play. • Are developing a strong sense of past and future. • Are able to cope with delay in having their needs met. • Show purpose and persistence and some control over their emotions. • Can be dogmatic and argumentative, and may blame others when they misbehave including provoking others in order to arouse a reaction. • May swear and use bad language. • May be able to feed themselves well, dress and undress, but may have difficulty with back buttons, ties and laces. • May be able to wash and dry hands and face and clean teeth.

continued

Age	Emotional and social development
5 years By this age children usually…	• Enjoy brief separations from home and carers. Show good overall control of emotions but may argue with parents when they request something. • Still respond to discipline based on bargaining, Are not so easily distracted from their own anger as when they were younger. • Want the approval of adults, show sensitivity to the needs of others and a desire for acceptance by other children. • Are developing internalised social rules, an inner conscience and a sense of shame (an important development that affects the adult's impact when disciplining the child). • They often show the stress of conflict by being overactive, but may regain their balance by having 'time-out'. • They prefer games of rivalry to team games. • Enjoy co-operative group play but often need an adult to sort out conflicts. • May boast, show off and threaten. • They are able to see a task through to the end. • Have developed a stable picture of themselves, are increasingly aware of differences between themselves and other people, including gender and status and want the approval of adults. They show sensitivity to the needs of others and a desire for acceptance by other children, and are developing internal social rules and inner conscience. • They may use a knife and fork well, dress and undress, lace shoes and tie ties, wash and dry face and hands but may need supervision to complete other washing.
6 years By this age children…	• Have greater independence and maturity. • Have developed a wide range of appropriate emotional responses. • Are able to behave appropriately in a variety of social situations. • Have all the basic skills for independence in eating, hygiene and toileting. • Can be irritable and possessive about their own things. • Have spells of being rebellious and aggressive.
7 years By this age children…	• Can be very self-critical about their work. • May be miserable and sulky, and give up trying for short periods, or be so enthusiastic for life that carers have to guard against them becoming overtired. • Are more aware of their gender group. • More influenced by the peer group.

Table 4.7 Emotional and social development: birth to seven years

The development of children's self-image

The development of children's self-image	
Age	**Developmental pattern**
Birth	• New-born babies do not realise that people and things exist apart and separate from them
1 month	• Children begin to learn to differentiate between themselves and other people through interaction with their carers and by exploration of the world through their senses. Through this they gradually come to a realisation of who they are and what they think and feel about themselves – their self-image and self-concept. This process begins around this age and continues right through childhood

2 months	• Babies learn that touching and seeing things around them feels completely different to touching their own hand. In feeling the difference they learn that that moving thing they see is somehow a part of them • When they are held during feeding, changing and cuddling, babies learn that there are different kinds of feeling; one that comes from outside of them; and another, when they touch their own hand or chew their toes, does not • These exploratory experiences begin the process of differentiation between themselves and other people and things
3 months	• Once children have distinguished themselves as separate they will start to build a picture or image of themselves. Gradually they discover what kind of person they are and what they can do • Children measure their worth by the responses of adults and other children who are significant to them. They need to experience the approval and acceptance of these people to develop feelings of self-approval and self-acceptance • At this stage infants still react to the world as if they alone make things exist or disappear: if they are looking at something it exists; if they don't see it, it doesn't exist. If someone disappears babies will keep looking for them in the place they were before they disappeared, as if waiting for them to come back. If they don't return the baby will probably not remember them unless it is a person who is important to them, in which case they will probably cry
6 months	• This period may see the beginnings of stranger anxiety and separation distress. This implies that the baby recognises their separateness and feels vulnerable without the support of the attachment relationship. If carers meet babies' needs at this stage they will reinforce the babies' view of themselves as separate but safe and worthwhile
9 months	• By this stage infants have become aware of themselves as separate from others and have formed a definite image of other people who are significant to them
12 months	• By this stage infants are aware of themselves as persons in relation to other people • Infants learn to feel about themselves what they see in the responses of others. This applies both to themselves and their activities and efforts. Children begin to feel positive about themselves if: adults are patient with their attempts to do things for themselves; they are allowed to explore and make new discoveries for themselves; they are allowed to attempt new physical skills without sensing fear from those around them • Infants' self-image is still fragile at this stage. Even if adults are generally encouraging and approving their moods can swing dramatically; powerful one moment, needy the next moment
18–24 months	• By this age some children have become sensitive to the feelings of others and display social emotions such as sympathy if a person is hurt. This implies that children understand how experiences make them feel and can recognise this in others (empathy), this is an indication of their growing self-awareness
2–3 years	• Children at this stage are developing personal independence and taking important steps towards self-reliance; with improved motor development children learn self-help skills. They will respond well if adults encourage this • Their developing competence confirms their self-worth • Adults can confirm children's separateness and individuality by, for example, setting things apart that belong to the child, a place to hang their coat or a cup that's theirs • Children need tasks that present manageable challenge and offer them opportunities for success and consequent enhancement of their self-esteem • Too much frustration and consequence at this stage can lead to a child feeling quite negative about themselves • It is particularly important to support children who have disabilities or learning difficulties at this stage to enable them to develop their sense of self-competence

continued

67

Age	Developmental pattern
3–4 years	• Between the ages of three and five the foundation of a child's self-concept is established • By three years old most children call themselves 'I' • Most children have a set of feelings about themselves • Their self-concept at this stage will influence how they respond to relationships and experiences now and in the future • Their view of themselves is still affected by the attitudes and behaviour of the people around them • Children see themselves as they think others see them
4–5 years	• Most children will have developed a stable self-concept • This will be based on their own inner understanding and knowledge about who they are • Children, who at this stage, see themselves as likeable will not change this view of themselves when, from time to time, other children say that they don't like them
6–7 years	• Much of the child's personality and sense of self is established by the end of this period. By the time they are eight, children's experiences in their families and in their social and cultural environments will have led to the establishment of their personal identity, social and cultural identity, gender role, attitudes to life, and skills for independence

Table 4.8 The development of children's self-image

The development of social play

The development of social play	
Solitary play	This is an early stage of play. Children play alone and take no notice of other children who are around
Parallel play	A child plays side-by-side with other child but without interacting. They may share space and possibly equipment but their play remains independent of one another
Associative play	Children begin to play with other children they make intermittent interactions and/or are involved in the same activity but their play remains predominantly personal
Co-operative play	At this stage children are able to play together co-operatively. They are able to adopt a role within a group and take account of others needs and actions. Children understand and are able to keep to simple rules in their play

Table 4.9 The development of social play

ACTIVITY 3

How would you encourage the development of children's social play from:

- *solitary to parallel;*

- *parallel to associative;*

- *associative to co-operative?*

Think about:

- *the activities and experiences that you could provide;*

- *how you would interact – including modelling play behaviour.*

Children's behaviour

Children's patterns of behaviour change as they grow and learn. Young children change dramatically in the first few years of their lives and this is reflected in their behaviour; this is an integral part of their ongoing emotional and social development. Throughout childhood children develop:

- an increasing range of emotions and behavioural responses to different situations;

- a greater degree of independence and control over their feelings and behaviour;

- a deeper understanding of feelings and behaviours of themselves and others, and therefore less need for external constrains on their behaviour.

Early Years practitioners need a thorough understanding of the behaviour to expect at each age and stage so that they can respond in an appropriate way, for example, a two year old throwing bricks down in frustration should be responded to differently than that same behaviour in a seven year old. When assessing children's behaviour early years practitioners need to consider whether the behaviour that they are observing is age appropriate, and develop strategies to manage each child's behaviour appropriately.

Children's behaviour	
Age	**Developmental pattern**
At one year	• Children do not have a clear picture of themselves as individuals • They have a close attachment, and are sociable with, the adults that they know and anxious if they are separated from familiar adults and shy with shy strangers • They are capable of varying emotional responses • They seek attention verbally • They will obey simple verbal instructions
At 15 months	• Children are more aware of themselves as individuals • They still do not see others as separate from themselves • They explore their environment indiscriminately (they are into everything) • They are possessive of people and things that they are attached to • They respond better to distraction than to verbal reasoning or sharp discipline • They may 'show off' their new-found skills and knowledge • Their mood can swing dramatically from anger to laughter in seconds • They are easily frustrated and may react by shouting and throwing things

continued

Age	Developmental pattern
At 18 months	• Children can respond to the work 'no', but will usually need the command repeated • They are more aware of themselves as separate individuals • They are very self-centred – or egocentric – in their awareness and behaviour • They are very curious about everything • They cannot tolerate frustration • They can be defiant and resistant to adults in order to protect their developing individuality
At 2 years	• Children have a clear understanding of self but are not yet fully aware of their carers as separate individuals • They are able to be self-contained for short periods of time • They are possessive of toys and have little idea of sharing • They want their demands to be met quickly • They may have tantrums if frustrated but can be distracted • They have a wide range of feelings and can be loving and responsive • They are aware of and are able to respond to the feelings of others
By the age of 3	• Children have developed a strong self-identity and a growing level of independence • They show less anxiety about separation and strangers • They often resist efforts by carers to limit their behaviour • They are ready to respond to reasoning and bargaining • They can wait for their needs to met • They are less rebellious and use language rather than physical outbursts to express themselves • They have mood swings and extremes of behaviour • They are impulsive and less easily distracted from what they want • They are beginning to learn appropriate behaviour for a range of different social settings • They can adopt the attitudes and moods of adults • They want approval from loved adults
By the age of 4	• Children have more physical and emotional self-control • They have more settled feelings and are more balanced in their expression of them • They are more independent of their main carers • They are more outwardly friendly and helpful • They can respond to reasoning and bargaining as well as distraction • They are less rebellious and can learn the appropriate behaviour for a range of settings • They are capable of playing with groups of children, tending to centre round an activity, then dissolve and reform • They can take turns but are not consistent at this • They can engage in elaborate and prolonged imaginary play • They are developing a sense of past and future • They can be dogmatic and argumentative • They may blame others when they misbehave • They may behave badly in order to get a reaction • They may swear and use bad language
Between 4 and 5 years	• Children are constantly trying to make sense of the world • They can be very sociable, talkative, confident, purposeful, persistent and self-assured • They can take turns and wait for their needs to be met • They may be stubborn and sometimes aggressive and argumentative • They still turn to adults for comfort, especially when tired, hurt, or ill

At 5 years	• Children have achieved a greater level of independence and self-containment • They generally show a well-developed level of control over their emotions • They show a desire to do well and to gain the approval of adults • They are developing a sense of shame if their behaviour is unacceptable to an adult • They can also be argumentative, show off, boast and be over reactive at times • They will argue with parents when they request something • They will still respond to discipline based on bargaining • They are not so easily distracted from their own anger as when they were younger • They may regain control by having 'time out' • They may prefer games of rivalry rather than team games • They enjoy co-operative group play but will often need an adult to arbitrate • They may boast, show off and threaten • They can show a desire to excel and be purposeful and persistent
Between 6 and 7 years	• Children become increasingly mature and independent • They develop a wide range of appropriate emotional and behavioural responses to different situations • They are able to behave appropriately in a variety of social settings • They can be self-confident, friendly and co-operative • They may have spells of being irritable, rebellious and sulky

Table 4.10 Children's behaviour

C H A P T E R   S U M M A R Y

This chapter identifies the principles underpinning children's development and learning. A series of detailed charts are provided detailing children learning and development from birth to seven in the areas of physical development, cognitive (or intellectual) development, language development, and emotional and social development.

FURTHER READING

Bruce, T and Meggitt, C (1999) *Childcare and education.* London: Hodder and Stoughton.

Empson, J and Nabuzoka, D with Hamilton, D (2004) *Atypical child development in context.* Basingstoke: Palgrave Macmillan.

Roberts, R (2002) *Self-esteem and early learning.* London: Paul Chapman Publishing.

Sheridan, M (1997 – revised and updated) *From birth to five years. Children's developmental progress.* London: Routledge.

Sylva, K, Meluish, E, Sammons, P, Siraj-Blatchford, I, Taggart, B and Elliot, K (2003) *Effective Provision of Pre-School Education (EPPE) Project: findings from the pre-school period.* **http://eppe.ioe. ac.uk/eppe/eppefindings.htm**

Tough, J (1976) *Listening to children talking.* East Grinstead: Ward Locke.

5 Development in the Early Years Foundation Stage

This chapter will enable you to understand:

- the background to the Early Years Foundation Stage (EYFS);
- the structure of the Early Years Foundation Stage;
- the Safeguarding and Welfare Standards;
- the way in which development is understood in the Early Years Foundation Stage;
- the way in which development is assessed in the Early Years Foundation Stage;
- expectations of Early Years practitioners in supporting Foundation Stage children's development;
- the ways in which development in the EYFS sits within a wider context of young children's learning and development.

Introduction: background to the EYFS

The Early Years Foundation Stage became statutory in September 2008 for all OFSTED registered Early Years providers. The framework brought together previous statutory care standards and curriculum guidance in one document. The framework was revised in 2011 and use of the new revised framework became statutory in September 2012.

The initial Early Years Foundation Stage formed part of the Every Child Matters agenda that sought to integrate services for children. It was an important part of the ten-year strategy for childcare: choice for parents, the best start for children. The aim in developing the Early Years Foundation Stage was to provide a single integrated framework for the care and education of children from birth to five years of age. The framework adopted a principled play-based approach to young children's learning and development. A review of the EYFS was undertaken by Dame Clare Tickell in 2011 as part of the agreed review of the framework at its inception. It was recognised that after a period of being used in settings the impact of the EYFS on children's outcomes and those working in the Foundation Stage should be evaluated. The review sought to build on what was working well, and address issues that had arisen. The review resulted in 46 recommendations which informed the revision of the EYFS. The revised framework (2012a) retains many aspects of the earlier framework including; a focus on an integrated framework for care and education of children from birth to five, a principled approach, and a strong emphasis on play and observation-based assessment.

Definitions	
Statutory	Required by law
Non-statutory	Not required by law

The structure of the Early Years Foundation Stage

The Early Years Foundation Stage is a framework that is built on the four themes:

- a unique child;

- positive relationships;

- enabling environments;

- learning and development.

See Table 5.1. Each theme has a guiding principle and these principles must inform the work of early years practitioners. Each of the principles is interpreted for practice in the documentation.

Theme	Principle	Practice
A unique child	Every child is a unique child who is constantly learning and can be resilient, capable, confident and self-assured	Practitioners • Understand and observe each child's development and learning, assess progress, plan for next steps • Support babies and children to develop a positive sense of their own identity and culture • Identify any need for additional support • Keep children safe • Value and respect all children and families equally
Positive relationships	Children learn to be strong and independent through positive relationships	Positive relationships are • Warm and loving and foster a sense of belonging • Sensitive and responsive to the child's needs, feelings and interests • Supportive of the child's own efforts and independence • Consistent in setting clear boundaries • Built on key person relationships in early years settings
Enabling environments	Children learn and develop well in enabling environments, in which their experiences respond to their individual needs and there is a strong partnership between practitioners and parents and carers	Enabling environments • Value all people • Value learning They offer • Stimulating resources relevant to all the children's cultures and communities • Rich learning opportunities through play and playful teaching • Support for children to take risks and explore
Learning and development	Children develop and learn in different ways. The framework covers the education and care of all children in early years provision, including children with special educational needs and disabilities	Practitioners teach children by ensuring challenging, playful opportunities across the prime and specific areas of learning and development They foster the characteristics of effective learning • Playing and exploring • Active learning • Creating and thinking critically

Table 5.1 EYFS: Four themes and principles
DFE (2012a)

The aim of these principles is to emphasise the holistic nature of children's development. The principles recognise that each child learns and develops in a unique context, and that that context includes the child themselves, the people with whom the child has relationships with, and the physical environment in which the child develops. These contexts are interdependent and will therefore have an important impact on each child's learning and development.

The first principle offers a really hopeful view of children. It recognises that all children, offered an appropriate context in which to grow and learn, can fulfil their potential. The principle emphasises the importance of practitioners understanding child development including how to promote children's self-identity and well-being and ensure that they are safe. The principle also recognises the importance of valuing and respecting all children and families to enable all children to achieve their potential.

The second principle recognises the importance of the social context in which children learn and grow. The importance of attachment is evident in the statement that, children grow and learn from a base of loving and secure relationships. This recognises the importance of strong, warm relationships within the home, and within settings, to enable children to fulfil their potential.

An effective learning environment is emphasised in the third principle. This principle recognises that access to a stimulating learning environment, both indoors and out, will be an important for a child's learning and development. It is important therefore that early years practitioners are knowledgeable about how young children grow and learn in order to provide an effective, enabling environment. The principle also highlights the importance of a playful teaching within a learning environment that supports and challenges children's instinct to explore their world. The importance of working with parents/carers is reiterated in this principle, recognising that an enabling environment extends beyond what happens in a setting.

The final principle emphasises the uniqueness of individual children and that individual experiences will mean that that they learn and develop in different ways. This is in accordance with developmental psychology that also emphasises the impact of children's experiences on their learning and development. Active learning through play and exploration are identified as the appropriate ways for young children to grow and learn.

These principles are supported with theory of how children develop and learn. They embed the work of Piaget, Vygotsky and Bowlby, and are supported by research that elucidates effective ways for children to learn, for example, the EPPE and REPEY projects.

Early Years Foundation Stage documentation

Documentation is provided for practitioners to enable them to meet the aims and requirements of the Early Years Foundation stage.

The statutory framework
The statutory framework is the legal framework for the Early Years Foundation Stage. Settings need to ensure that they comply with the framework in order to meet the legal

requirements of running a setting. This means ensuring that the setting has the necessary policies and procedures in place, and, that staff are sufficiently well trained to understand, teach, plan and assess children's learning in each area of learning.

- **The learning and development requirements**
  The framework outlines the seven areas of learning and development that must shape the educational programmes in early years settings. It lists the early learning goals that apply in each of the areas of learning.

- **Assessment**
  This section outlines how assessment should be undertaken in the Foundation Stage. It identifies ongoing observation-based assessment as the way to understand children's needs and inform provision and practice. The section also outlines the two points in the Foundation Stage when practitioners must make summative assessments of children's learning, and how these assessments must be used to inform parents about their child's progress and, at the end of Foundation Stage, reported to teachers and to the local authority.

- **The safeguarding and welfare requirements**
  These are a series of legal requirements that state what practitioners must do to safeguard and support young children's welfare.

Development in the Early Years Foundation Stage

In support of the statutory framework practitioners are offered further guidance on understanding young children's learning and development in the non-statutory guidance *Development Matters in the Early Years Foundation Stage* (DFE, 2012b).

Development matters

The document provides guidance on:

- interpreting the themes and principles of the EYFS;

- formative and summative assessment;

- developmental parameters in each area of learning from birth to the end of the Foundation Stage.

Developmental matters guidance charts
The development matters guidance charts outline sequences against which children's learning can be mapped, and the next stage in learning identified. Each area of learning identifies developmental progress towards stated Early Learning Goals (ELG). The Early Learning Goals are statements of the developmental level, in each of the seven areas of learning, to be reached by the end of the Foundation Stage. It is a requirement of the EYFS that children's development towards the early learning goals is tracked and parents informed of their child's progress. However, the guidance is not a curriculum that has to be followed. It is a framework for understanding the developmental sequences of

knowledge, skills and aptitudes that are likely to enable a child to reach the early learning goals by the time that they reach the end of the Foundation Stage.

It is important to be aware that stating learning requirements and outcomes for our youngest children, linked to ages and stages, is a controversial issue. It is only in recent years that there have been stated outcomes for these children. Many people believe that the way in which very young children grow and learn doesn't fit with the idea of formalising the patterns and aims of their learning at such a young age, and that education for young children should be constructed very differently to later school-based learning.

ACTIVITY 1

Investigate the controversy around the idea of stated learning outcomes for very young children.

- *What are the reasons for having stated learning goals for young children?*

- *What are the arguments against this?*

- *What is your view?*

The Development Matters charts are from birth to five years old and are organised in six different age ranges within seven areas of learning.

The areas of learning are divided into two sections.

- Prime areas: Personal, Social and Emotional Development; Communication and Language; Physical Development.

- Specific areas: Literacy; Maths; Understanding the World; Expressive Arts and Design.

Each area of learning has a series of sub-sections called aspects (Table 5.2).

These identified stages in these developmental charts are intended to support practitioners' interpretation of their observations and help them to define children's next steps in learning. This is important. The charts are not a series of learning outcomes to be taught. They should be used as a reference to assist in the assessment of what children know and can do. Once this is established the charts can then be used to inform 'what next?' as a basis for further play-based provision to enhance learning and development. The advice throughout the documentation is clear:

> Children develop at their own rates, and in their own ways. The development statements and their order should not be taken as necessary steps for individual children. They should not be used as checklists.

> (DfE, 2012b, p.6)

Prime area of learning	Aspect
Personal, Social and Emotional Development	Making relationships Self-confidence and self-awareness Managing feelings and behaviour
Physical Development	Moving and handling Health and self-care
Communication and Language	Listening and attending Understanding Speaking
Specific area of learning	**Aspect**
Literacy	Reading Writing
Maths	Numbers Shape, space and measure
Understanding the World	People and communities The world Technology
Expressive Arts and Design	Exploring and using media and materials Being imaginative

Table 5.2 Prime areas and specific areas of learning (and aspects)

ACTIVITY 2

Refer back to Chapter 3 Holistic development.

- *What are the inconsistencies between a holistic view of children's learning and dividing learning into areas of learning, development charts and learning outcomes?*

- *In what ways can practitioners provide for this in their settings, recognising that young children's learning is holistic whilst meeting the requirements of the EYFS?*

The age ranges

There are six stated age ranges in the development matters charts. You will notice that the age ranges overlap. This reflects the emphasis on tracking developmental progress in the EYFS rather than focusing on age related milestones. Each child should be regarded as an individual who is likely to have slightly different pattern of development across the areas of learning. The documentation states this explicitly.

> *The age/stage bands overlap because these are not fixed age boundaries but sugge* *typical range of development.*

(DfE, 20

ACTIVITY 3

Reflect on the three aspects of the Early Years Foundation Stage listed below.

- *The EYFS development matters guidance states:* children develop at their own rates and in their own ways;

- *There is an expectation that most children will achieve the Early Learning Goals by the time they reach the end of the Foundation Stage;*

- *The developmental charts are written linked to broad ages and stages.*

What are the implications of this for early years practice?

Further support for provision

The developmental charts also offer ways to understand what the requirements of the EYFS look like in practice. The charts identify what practitioners can do, and what they can provide, in addition to what can be observed as evidence of development.

The first column on each page identifies what practitioners may observe as evidence of what a child knows and can do. This is progressive listing of what may be observed from birth to five years of age. The second column offers advice about positive relationships: what practitioners can do to facilitate a child's learning in the area at that particular stage of development. Column three offers advice on enabling environments: what adults can provide to support learning and development in the area of learning at that stage of learning.

Assessment and reporting of development in the EYFS

Assessment of children's learning at Foundation Stage must be based on practitioners' observations of what children do when engaged in day-to-day play activities. This is called observation-based assessment, and should form the basis of all assessment in the EYFS. All adults involved with the child should be able contribute to this process, including parents. Practitioners need to involve, and take note of, parents' contributions to the assessment of their child's learning. This ongoing assessment to inform practice is called formative assessment.

Additionally all providers must report progress and achievements to parents, teachers and other authorities during the Foundation Stage. These are summative assessments. This means that a child's progress is identified and recorded at a single point in time. This happens twice in the Foundation Stage, namely:

- a progress check at age two;

- the Early Years Foundation Stage Profile at age five.

The progress check at age two

The progress check at age two is an addition in the 2012 revised framework. The review can be undertaken anytime between 24 and 36 months but, where possible, in time to inform the Healthy Child Programme health and development review that health visitors undertake at age two.

It requires that practitioners review and make a summative assessment of a child's progress in the prime areas of learning. The review must identify the child's strengths and any areas where the child's progress is less than expected. If there are significant emerging concerns, or an identified special needs or disability, practitioners must, in partnership with parents, identify a targeted plan for support.

Practitioners must provide a short written summary of their child's progress to parents. The summary must have information on areas in which the child is progressing well and areas in which some additional support might be needed across the three prime areas of learning. Where additional support is required the summary must describe the activities and strategies that are going to be put in place to support the child's learning. This may include seeking support of other professionals outside the setting. Providing that these aspects are included practitioners can decide on any other information to be included.

It is important to be aware that intervention to support learning is best achieved when parents and settings work together. Therefore, if there is cause for concern with a child's progress in the progress check at age two then it is good practice to involve parents in discussions and decisions about how to support the child's learning. If advice or support is sought from outside agencies, such a speech and language therapist, the setting then has a duty to seek consent from parents to begin this process. Settings cannot act to involve other agencies without this consent, unless the issues are ones of safeguarding.

The Early Years Foundation Stage Profile

In addition to the progress check at age two there is a requirement to complete The Early Years Foundation Stage Profile (EYFSP) in the final term of the year in which the child reaches five years. For most children this will be at the end of the Reception year in school, although some children may still be in early childhood settings such as day nurseries. The assessment must reflect ongoing observation-based assessment of the child and discussions with parents and other adults involved with the child. The profile assesses a child's progress against the Early Learning Goals (ELG). Practitioners must make a judgement about whether children are not yet meeting expected levels of development (emerging), meeting expected levels of development, or if they are exceeding expected levels.

The profile must be completed for all children, including those with special educational needs or disabilities. The framework states that 'reasonable adjustments' to the assessment process must be made for these children. This may involve seeking specialist advice or assistance to understand what reasonable adjustments need to be, depending on the child's needs.

Outcomes from the EYFSP must be shared with parents, given to year one teachers and submitted to local authorities. The local authority collects and collates data and returns it to the relevant government department.

ACTIVITY **4**

- List other things that practitioners and parents may want to know or find out about their children in addition to their developmental progress as outlined in the EYFS.

- What are the benefits of knowing these other things about the child for:

  – the child;

  – the practitioner;

  – the parents/carers?

In what ways does this reflect a holistic understanding of young children's learning and development?

The safeguarding and welfare requirements

In addition to expectations for children's learning, the Statutory Framework sets out the legal requirements relating to children's welfare. These are called the safeguarding and welfare requirements. The requirements state what providers must do to ensure that children in their care are safe and that they promote children's health and well-being. They are divided into a number of sections; each of which has clear guidance about what providers must do to meet the requirements. The areas are:

- child protection;

- suitable people;

- health;

- managing behaviour;

- safety and suitability of premises, environment and equipment;

- equal opportunities;

- information and record.

It is important that all early years practitioners know what the safeguarding and welfare standards are, how they are embedded in policy, and how they are implemented in practice. It is the responsibility of individual staff members as well as the management in a setting to ensure that all practitioners know what the policies and procedures are that enable a setting to fulfil their legal responsibilities. There are many day-to-day procedures in a setting that you will need to be aware of and to follow when required, for example, as a member of staff you will need to know: the procedures for reporting any safeguarding concerns that you may have; you will need to the rules on administering medicine to children; what to do if a child isn't collected at the end of a session; and how to maintain the necessary documentation to record these events.

Expectations of EYFS practitioners

The Early Years Foundation Stage has a series of expectations about practice during the Foundation Stage. It is expected that learning and development will be facilitated through play. This should be a balance of child-initiated and adult-led activities and experiences. It is expected that practitioners will work in partnership with parents. This recognises the important role that parents have in supporting their child's learning and development. Also, it is expected that practitioners will work, where appropriate, with other professionals who are involved in supporting children's development, for example, speech and language therapists or educational psychologists. Practice at Foundation Stage should also promote equality of opportunity. This means removing barriers where they exist; being alert to the signs of needs and responding quickly and appropriately; respecting all children irrespective of background; and stretching and challenging all children to achieve their potential.

C H A P T E R   S U M M A R Y

In this chapter we have seen how the Early Years Foundation Stage is part of the government's agenda to integrate childcare and education from birth to five years. This had its roots in the aims of Every Child Matters and formed part of the ten-year childcare strategy. It has been shown that the EYFS is a principle-based framework, and the principles have been outlined. The structure of the framework has been explained including an overview of the safeguarding and welfare standards. We have seen that the 'development matters' charts are a tool for tracking children's development towards the Early Learning Goals. This is important to understand. They are not intended as a series of learning outcomes to be taught but a reference to understand each child's developmental progress. Observation-based assessment has been identified as the way in which early years practitioners must assess children's developmental progress. It is an important aspect of the framework that parents contribute to the assessment of their child and that they are kept informed about their child's progress towards the Early Learning Goals. It has been seen that there are expectations that practitioners will provide play-based learning, that they will work in partnership with parents, and, that practitioners will ensure equality of opportunity in which they work closely with parents and other professionals to provide the best chances for young children to achieve their potential. Throughout the chapter you have been asked to consider the ways in which development, as understood in the EYFS, sits within a wider context of understandings of children's learning and development.

FURTHER READING

Beckley, P, Elvige, K and Hendry, H (2009) *Implementing the Early Years Foundation Stage. A handbook.* Buckingham: Open University Press.

DFE (2012a) *Early Years Foundation Stage.* **www.education.gov.uk/schools/ teachingandlearning/curriculum/a0068102/early-years-foundation-stage-eyfs**

DFE (2012b) *Development matters in the Early Years Foundation Stage.* **http://media.education.gov. uk/assets/files/pdf/d/development%20matters%20in%20the%20eyfs.pdf**

Every Child Matters (2004) **https://www.education.gov.uk/publications/standard/ publicationDetail/Page1/DfES/1081/2004**

Moyles, J (2007) *Early Years Foundation Stage. Meeting the challenge.* Buckingham: Open University Press.

Tailent, L and Reed, K (2010) *A step-by-step guide to the EYFS. How to make sense of the EYFS.* London: Featherstone Publications.

Tassoni, P (2008) *Penny Tassoni's practical EYFS handbook.* London: Heinemann.

Wilcock, I and Hughes, C (2009) *The Early Years Foundation Stage in practice.* London: Step Forward Publishing.

6 Factors affecting children's learning and development

This chapter enables you to understand:

- the different factors that affect children's development;
- why it is important that society supports all children's learning and development;
- how inclusive practices can support the development of all children.

Introduction

Children's development occurs through a complex patterning of biological unfolding and the social context in which a child grows and learns. For most children this process results in development progress being within established developmental parameters. However, for some children there are factors in their lives that mean that their development is affected. For some children the social context of their lives affects their development. For some children their development is atypical because of a biological condition. For others, a combination of biological and social factors affect their development.

Definition	
Established developmental parameters	Agreed and established expectations of physical, intellectual, linguistic, emotional and social development at a given chronological age

Children's developmental progress requires additional consideration when their development falls outside of expectations. For some children this will be that their development exceeds established developmental expectations. Within settings these children must be identified and their needs met through additional or enhanced provision. Other children's development will fall below established expectations. Again, these children's needs need to be identified and met if they are to fulfil their potential.

Factors affecting development

Look carefully at Figure 6.1. It shows the relative impact of genetic (biological) and environmental (social) factors on physical, linguistic, cognitive (intellectual), social and emotional development. It is important to understand that these are only relative to one another; there is, as yet, no definitive understanding of the actual relative impact of the biological imperative and social learning on children's development. The diagram shows the general principle that both biology (potentials that we are born with) and social experiences (the sum of our experiences after we are born) influence our development, and that the balance of this is different in different areas of development.

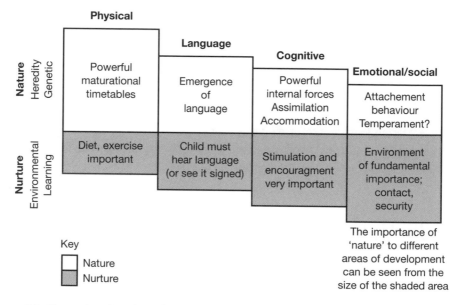

Figure 6.1 Chart showing the relative influence of nature and nurture on different developmental areas

The impact of social and emotional factors on learning and development

When children's emotional needs are not met within the social context of their lives this has been shown to impact on their development. The impact is likely to be greatest initially in the areas of social and emotional development and this is then likely to have an impact on other aspects of their development.

The impact of children's needs not being met within the social context of their lives is borne out by the evidence. It is known that many children who have difficult life circumstances: for example, children in care, children who suffer abuse and neglect (safeguarding issues), children who suffer from discrimination, all suffer distress that is, in turn, likely to have an impact on their development.

The human givens approach

The human givens approach offers a way of understanding why when children's needs are not met, it can affect their development. The approach holds that we are born with a range of needs both physical and emotional. These needs, it is argued, are innate, they have evolved over millions of years and exist whatever our cultural background. They are a common human biological inheritance – hence 'human givens'. When most of these physical and emotional needs are met we survive and develop as individual and as a species. In contrast, when too many of these needs are not met we suffer distress. This distress is an indication that our needs are not being met and this has an impact on ourselves and the people around us.

THEORY FOCUS

Human givens

Given physical needs: As animals we are born into a world where we need air to breathe, water, nutritious food and sufficient sleep. These are the paramount physical needs. Without them, we quickly die. We also need to be able to stimulate our senses and exercise our muscles. These physical needs are intimately bound up with our emotional needs which are the main focus of human givens psychology.

Given emotional needs: Emotions create distinctive psychological and biological states within us and drive us to take action. The emotional needs that are programmed within us are there to connect us to the world and to other people, and to survive in it. These needs seek fulfilment through the way we interact in the world. Consequently, when these needs are not met, nature ensures that we suffer considerable distress as an indication that our needs are not being met. This results in behaviour that impacts upon ourselves and the people around us.

There is widespread agreement as to the nature of our emotional needs. The main ones are listed below.

Emotional needs include:

- security – a safe environment which allows us to develop fully;

- attention – to give and receive it;

- sense of autonomy and control;

- emotional intimacy – knowing that at least one other person accepts us totally for who we are;

continued

- feeling part of a wider community;

- privacy;

- sense of status within social groupings;

- sense of competence and achievement;

- meaning and purpose – which come from being stretched in what we do and think.

Adapted from **www.hgi.org.uk**

The human givens approach offers a way of understanding what children's emotional needs are and, therefore, a way of understanding why, when these needs are not met children are adversely affected. The approach offers a framework for understanding and interpreting children's distress.

The approach also offers a framework for working with children adversely affected by their life experiences. An understanding of human givens provides a framework for understanding children's needs and therefore, possible interventions to meet these needs and support children's social and emotional development.

ACTIVITY 2

Read through the list of emotional needs in the human givens approach.

- *In what ways can these needs be met in children's families?*

- *How can they be met within an early years setting?*

- *How might this understanding help you to understand the needs of children whose development is affected by their life experiences?*

- *How may an understanding of the human givens approach contribute to early years practitioners' knowledge and skills?*

It is apparent, from research and data, that there are a number of different social and cultural factors that affect children's learning and development. It can be observed that there are patterns of underachievement for children from certain identifiable groups. The development of many of these children, in different ways, falls outside of expected parameters. The reasons for this are many and complex but undoubtedly social and cultural factors have an impact on children's learning and development. This can be both a positive and a negative effect. Nutbrown and Clough (2006) identify a range of areas which are known to have an impact on issues of inclusion and exclusion within education and society (Table 6.1).

Areas of inclusion/exclusion	
• Challenging behaviour	• Physical impairment
• Disability	• Poverty
• Emotional and behavioural difficulty	• Race/ethnicity
• Employment status	• Religion
• Gender	• Sexual orientation
• Housing	• Social class
• Language	• Special educational needs
• Mental health	

Table 6.1 Areas of inclusion/excusion within education and society

There is ongoing debate and concern about the disparity in school attainment, and the associated benefits, between certain identifiable groups within society. This is often cause for sensationalist headlines both in the political world and the media. However, the reality is more complex. It is true that at a very generalised level we can comment on the overall attainment of children from particular societal groups, and this is perhaps necessary when making strategic decisions about provision and funding. However, equally important is the realisation that these are quite unsubtle categories and, when we compare like with like, a different picture emerges; for example, there is currently concern about the apparent underachievement of boys in the education system, however, Skelton, Francis and Valkanova (2007) found that social class is a stronger factor in achievement than gender regardless of ethnic group. This doesn't mean that there aren't specific groups that will require targeted support but to recognise that the headlines may not always be supported by the subtleties in the facts.

ACTIVITY 3

Find out about one of the areas of inclusion/exclusion listed above.

• *What is the impact on children's learning and development?*

• *What are the suggested social and/or cultural reasons for this impact on learning and development?*

• *How can Early Years provision ameliorate the impact on children whose learning and development is affected by social and cultural factors in their lives? Think about:*

– *work with individual children;*

– *work with parents;*

– *developing practice to promote attitudes of equality and social cohesion.*

Children living in poverty

One of the most significant factors affecting children's learning and development is growing up in an area of social deprivation. Evidence also shows that many children who grow up in poverty are adversely affected by their life experiences. The relationship between deprivation and education is well documented and affects a significant number of children in our society. Deprivation has a negative impact on educational attainment. In the long term children who grow up in poverty leave school with fewer qualifications and skills, which in turn affects jobs and employment. Poverty is linked to poorer health and a negative impact on engagement with society; for example, an increased likelihood that an individual will engage in criminal activity (DCSF, 2009). The disparity in attainment is described as substantial and pervasive from an early age (DCSF, 2009). Studies on young children's development show that there were differences in cognitive development of children from different socio-economic groups as young as 22 months. Other studies have shown that even when the development of children from lower socio-economic groups met developmental expectations at 22 months by the time they entered primary school they had been overtaken by others (Feinstein, 2003). Foundation Stage Profile scores completed at the end of Reception year in school consistently confirms this disparity in attainment as children reach compulsory school age. Evidence shows that this disparity continues throughout schooling for children living in poverty. It is difficult to explain exactly why this happens but there are a range of social factors that can be identified as being significant in the association between deprivation and poor educational outcomes (DCSF, 2009).

Income and material deprivation

A low income has been shown to mean a lack of access to books, computers and other reading materials and space to study quietly. It affects the quality of the home environment and neighbourhood as low income restricts where families can live. There may be no quiet spaces to work or sleep and this has an impact on emotional well-being. Children's diets may be inadequate because of lack of money, and poor nutrition can lead to physical changes that affect cognitive ability and performance of the brain (DCSF, 2009).

Health

Low birth weight is more likely in children from lower socio-economic groups and this is associated with risks to cognitive and physical development throughout childhood. Poorer children are likely to suffer poorer health throughout their childhood including chronic illness (CPAG, 2009).

Family stress

Poverty and deprivation have an indirect impact on children's outcomes because of family stress and parenting practices. Low income leads to economic hardship which tends to have a negative impact on parents' well-being and this means that they are less likely to be able to provide warm supportive parenting. This can lead to problems with children's emotional and social development and thus their educational achievement.

Parental education

The level of parents' achievement is strongly associated with children's outcomes (Hobbs, 2003). Higher levels of parental education have been shown to have a positive effect on factors such as income, health, levels of familial stress and resilience and on the interactions within the family that support children's development.

Parental involvement in their children's education

Parental involvement takes many forms and has been shown to have a positive impact on children's development: provision of a stable and secure environment, intellectual stimulation, parent–child discussion, good models of valuing education, high aspirations, contact with and participation in the work and life of the school. Families with low incomes are more likely to have had negative experiences of school themselves and may be reluctant to become involved. These experiences may be also result in them not having the knowledge and skills and to help and support their children's learning.

Cultural and social capital, and the experience of schooling

Some research has suggested that a lack of social and cultural capital leads to low attainment for children living in poverty. It is suggested that children from lower socio-economic groups have different background knowledge skills and interests that aren't reflected in the school curriculum. These differences in cultural capital mean that the curriculum is more difficult for these children to access. The Social Exclusion Task Force (SETF) (2008) reported that young people in deprived communities often lack social capital: access to sources of inspiration, role models, support and opportunity and, even those children with high aspirations were found to lack the understanding about what to do to achieve their goals.

Children from deprived backgrounds were also found to have a particular negative perception of schools as controlling and coercive (Hirsch, 2007). They are reported as feeling under pressure to perform tasks in which they lacked confidence and as experiencing a sense of worthlessness (Reay, 2006).

Definition	
Cultural capital	The capacity for individuals to understand the dominant culture within society and use the language and behaviours associated with it
Social capital	Having contacts and being part of social groups and networks that enable access to support and resources

Low aspiration

Children from deprived backgrounds are less likely than their peers to hold high aspirations for their future. The strongest factors affecting levels of children's aspiration are: the value they attach to school, belief in their ability, attainment, mother's aspiration for the child to go to university, and socio-economic status (SETF, 2008).

Exposure to multiple risk factors

Living in a low-income household or a deprived area makes it more likely that children will be exposed to one or more risk factors that affect their life chances. Risk factors include: depression, illness, smoking during pregnancy, alcohol abuse, domestic violence, financial stress, worklessness, teenage parenthood, lack of basic skills, and overcrowding.

Literacy

Children from the poorest backgrounds typically have the poorest literacy skills from an early age and fewer opportunities outside school to develop their literacy. Levels of literacy have a direct impact on learning and development. They are a prerequisite for accessing the curriculum at all levels.

THEORY FOCUS

32 million fewer words

> Why will some children arrive in kindergarten having heard 32 million fewer words then their classmates? (Hart and Risley, 1995)

Hart and Risley (1995) sought to understand why some children, even when they learn to say their first words at the same age as other children, were much slower to develop their language and their development was forever in the shadow of other children.

Their research drew three important conclusions.

- There were significant differences in the amount of talking that goes on in families. In an average hour some adults spent more than 40 minutes interacting with their children, others less than 15 minutes. Some parents responded more than 250 times to their children, others less than 15. Some parents expressed approval and encouragement of their child's actions more than 40 times an hour, other less than 4 times. Some parents said more than 3000 words per hour to their child in an average hour, others fewer than 500 words. The data showed that the amount of talk was so consistent over time that the differences in the child's language experience mounted up month by month, so, by the age of three years old, the differences were immense.

- These differences in language experiences were closely linked to significant differences in outcomes for the child.

- The quality and type of interaction in the home was also significant in outcomes for the child. All parents used a similar number of imperatives ('come here') and prohibitions ('stop that') and question ('what are you doing?'). However, the data showed that when parents engaged children in more talk than was necessary to communicate these imperatives, prohibitions and questions the quality of the talk changed considerably. Parents moved into discussing feelings, plans, present activities, past events and the vocabulary became more varied and the descriptions richer and more nuanced. Their talk also became more positive and responsive to their child (Hart and Risley, 1995).

By as early as the age of three the children's talk had come to match that of the adults. By three children were talking as much – but only as much – as their parents were. Furthermore, the children's talk was as varied – but only as varied as their parents' (Hart and Risley, 1995).

Hart and Risley (1995) conclude that the most important aspect of a child's language development is the amount of language that children hear. This, they argue, holds important lessons for early language intervention programmes.

It is important to be aware that not all children who live in deprived areas will be affected. Children must be regarded as individuals not as representative of groups to which they belong. Similarly, there will be children who live in more affluent areas whose development falls below established expectations. As Sylva et al. (2004) concluded, for all children the home learning environment is more important for intellectual and social development than parental occupation, education or income. What parents do is more important than who they are.

However, despite this assertion, the evidence shows that many children and their families who live in poverty are likely to need focused support in their Early Years and during schooling if their development is to remain within established developmental parameters (Washbrook and Waldfogel, 2010).

ACTIVITY *4*

The impact on educational attainment and children's life chances of living in poverty is well established, and, because of this, there are a range of initiatives in Early Years intended to support children and families living in deprived areas and ameliorate the effects of poverty.

- *Read through the list of social factors that are known to have an impact on children's educational attainment.*

- *Investigate the initiatives in early years that have been established to support young children and their families. The first section of this book, 'Early childhood context and policy', outlines some of the initiatives.*

- *Find out what the impact of these initiatives has been.*

- *Why do you think that it is important that, as a society, we support these young children and their families?*

Other factors affecting children's learning and development: children who have special educational needs

The development of children who are regarded as having special educational needs is likely to be atypical. That means that a child's development does not follow expected patterns and/or profiles. Individual children's development will be affected in different ways depending upon the nature of their abilities and needs. There will be a wide range of needs amongst children. Some children's needs will be pervasive and lifelong, other children may require time limited interventions to support their development and learning.

The aim of all Early Years practitioners who work with children who have special educational needs must be to understand each child as an individual and to support their development as necessary. This must begin with what the child knows and can do as the basis for support and intervention. As Bissex (1980) observes, it is an inescapable fact the only place to start to work out how we can best support children's learning is to start from the child. Starting from the child is particularly important when working with children who have special educational needs. Each one of these children will have a different profile of abilities and needs and, in order to best support their learning and development, these abilities and needs must be understood and appropriate provision made to enable them to fulfil their potential.

Why it is important that society supports all children's learning and development?

Supporting the learning and development of all children according to need is a cornerstone of our care and education systems. It is an issue of rights; the right of all children to be treated with equal value and respect and offered the opportunity to flourish and make a contribution to society. However, within our society it is recognised that not all children start from an equal position and so don't have the same access to opportunities within society. It is a reality that, within our society, some groups and individuals are advantaged whilst others are disadvantaged and/or discriminated against (Kahn and Young, 2007). Therefore, it is important that as a society we aim to recognise, understand, remove and help children overcome barriers to reaching their potential. These decisions are underpinned by a number of moral, ethical and political choices that determine what kind of society it is that we want to build.

The issue of supporting all children's learning and development within Early Years settings, schools and the wider society is referred to as inclusion. Inclusion began as an issue specifically related to children who have special education needs, and their right to be educated in mainstream schools alongside their siblings and peers. However, the current interpretation of inclusion has been extended to include all children who are potentially disenfranchised within society (Nutbrown and Clough, 2006).

Inclusion is not about treating everyone in the same way. It is about recognising that there are barriers to some children's learning and development and, in different ways, supporting these children to reach their potential. Inclusion is about putting into practice the moral and political choices that have been made to create a society which values every child and offers every child the opportunity to flourish.

Supporting the development of all children: inclusion for children with special educational needs

Historically, many children whose development was considered to be outside of expected developmental parameters were segregated into schools for children regarded as having learning difficulties. From the early 1990s onwards the appropriateness of having this separate system for children with special educational needs was challenged, predominately as a human rights issue (Farrell and Ainscow, 2002). The opening up of this debate had a powerful effect on the processes and thinking in society around disability and children who have special educational needs. It resulted in the development of new ideas and approaches to the education of all children: a commitment to inclusive education which is now embedded in legislation and guidance.

The United Nations Convention on the Rights of the Child, ratified by the UK government in 1991, affords children a series of rights. The convention is built around four guiding principles: non-discrimination, the best interests of the child, optimal development, the voice of the child. Each one of these principles can provide a powerful argument for the inclusion of children with special educational needs in mainstream school.

ACTIVITY 5

Investigate the principles and stated rights of United Nations Convention on the Rights of the Child.

- *In what way can these rights be used to argue for the inclusion of most children in their local school?*

- *In what situations might this not be possible? In these cases what else could be done to ensure that children are not discriminated against, that their best interests are taken into account, and that their development is optimised?*

In June 1994 the world conference on special education needs held in Salamanca in Spain called for inclusive education to be the norm. The guiding principle of this was that children should go to local schools regardless of their physical, intellectual, linguistic, social or emotional needs. The statement asked that governments give high financial and political priority to improving educational services so that all children could be included in local schools, regardless of difference or difficulty. The Salamanca framework begins with a statement outlining the benefits of a commitment to education for all.

> *Regular schools with this inclusive orientation are the most effective means of combating discriminatory attitudes, creating welcoming communities, building an inclusive society and achieving education for all; moreover, they provide an effective education to the majority of children and improve the efficiency and ultimately the cost-effectiveness of the entire education system.*

UNESCO Salamanca Agreement

In 1997 the government published a paper *Excellence for all Children* in which they outlined their commitment to promoting the inclusion of children with special educational needs in mainstream, local schools alongside their peers. They argued that there are strong reasons for educating all children together wherever possible. They state that this issue is one of civil rights for disabled people: that our nation's aspirations must be for all people.

The right to an inclusive education is now embedded the United Nations Convention on the Rights of Persons with Disabilities, which was ratified by the UK in 2009.

Article 24 of the United Nations Convention on the Rights of Persons with Disabilities states that:

Governments must ensure an inclusive education system at all levels directed to:

- *the full development of human potential and sense of dignity and self-worth, and the strengthening of respect for human rights, fundamental freedoms and human diversity;*

- *the development by persons with disabilities of their personality, talents and creativity, as well as their mental and physical abilities, to their fullest potential;*

- *enabling persons with disabilities to participate effectively in a free society.*

To achieve this governments must ensure that:

- *persons with disabilities are not excluded from the general education system on the basis of disability, and that children with disabilities are not excluded from free and compulsory primary education, or from secondary education, on the basis of disability;*

- *persons with disabilities can access an inclusive, quality and free primary education and secondary education on an equal basis with others in the communities in which they live.*

A social model of disability

Another powerful argument for an inclusive approach to children who have special educational needs is one based upon a social model of disability. The social model of disability turns conventional reasoning on its head. It argues that the reason that some people are unable to participate fully in society is not because of their own individual needs but because processes within society, attitudes and provision, make their full participation impossible. It is argued that discriminatory attitudes in society towards difference leads to exclusion. Similarly, provision that means that people cannot gain access to public spaces or services because of their needs automatically excludes some people from full participation. Therefore, the way in which society is currently constructed, disables some people. The social model of disability argues that addressing issues of disability must start with the barriers in attitudes and provision being removed to enable all people to participate fully in society.

An inclusive approach to the care and education of young children is part of the approach. Inclusive practice can build communities where all people are accepted, where difference is an everyday part of life, and where provision is organised and constructed to enable all children and their families to participate. So, what is inclusive practice? What does it mean for practice in early years? How does it support the learning and development of all children in our society?

Picture a cartoon. In it a man is clearing snow from the steps of a school building. A pupil in a wheelchair asks whether the man can clear the snow from the ramp that runs alongside the steps. The man replies that the children are waiting so he'll clear the ramp once he has finished clearing the steps. The pupil in the wheelchair replies that if the man clears the snow from the ramp then everyone can use the ramp to get into school.

- *What is the barrier to everyone's full participation?*

- *In what ways does it prevent everyone participating fully?*

- *How can this barrier be overcome?*

- *What can we learn from this example about building an inclusive society where everyone is able to participate fully?*

- *Can you think of more examples like this?*

Inclusive practice

What is inclusive practice?

Having an inclusive approach is about attitudes and practices. In Early Years this means that all practitioners must be committed to ensuring that their provision does not exclude anyone, and that each child's learning and development is supported according to need.

- Practitioners' attitudes towards others must be without prejudice.

- As far as possible practitioners must ensure that provision can accessed by all children and families.

- Practice must anticipate and take account of differences in need, and provide for this.

- This approach should inform all that practitioners do.

There are two main aspects of inclusive provision.

- That overall, daily provision should be as accessible as possible to all children and families.

- That additional support should be provided for children who need it.

CASE STUDY

Phoebe had taken over the leadership of Butts Lane playgroup. She had recently started working towards becoming an Early Years Professional and, as part of the process, was becoming increasingly aware of the need to ensure that the provision in the playgroup was inclusive. She decided to start by focusing on the continuous provision. Alongside staff Phoebe looked closely at the provision in the group and found many aspects of practice and provision that worked well.

- *The books reflected the diversity in society and they had a good range of fact and fiction books.*
- *Visual timetables were used to support routines for all children and enhance provision for children who needed additional support.*
- *They organised the room well each day with a wide range of activities provided in different ways and with sufficient space to move around the room.*
- *The role play area and equipment reflected diverse traditions in family life.*
- *Staff used Makaton signs alongside speaking as a support to communication during child-initiated and adult-led activities and group times.*
- *They provided story sacks and a toy library for the children to borrow books and toys so that families could enjoy playing and reading together at home.*

The staff agreed that they could make their provision even better if they observed the following.

- *Symbols were used as visual prompts at group times more consistently (see below). This would support all children's understanding of the behavioural expectations at group times.*
- *Provision and interaction actively encouraged children to engage with activities that they didn't readily choose. They decided to start with encouraging the boys to do more mark making. They had noticed that they enjoyed playing at police and arresting one another. So the staff decided to join in the play and encourage the boys to record what had happened in notebooks.*

The staff implemented these changes and agreed to review them six weeks later to evaluate whether these changes had been effective in developing inclusive practice in the playgroup.

Definitions	
Makaton	A communication technique that uses speech, facial expression, gestures, signs and symbols to communicate. It can be used as a multi-dimensional way of learning to communicate and as a way of communicating for people who have communication needs.
Story sacks	A bag containing a book with games and props linked to the story. The aim is engage children and their families in story reading, story-telling and playing together.
Symbols	A picture/graphic to represent a word. They offer a visual support to understanding.
Mark making	The marks children make to graphically represent their ideas, thoughts and feelings. Through these representations children communicate their ideas, express their feelings and develop their ideas; they record and make their understanding and thinking visible to other people.

CASE STUDY continued

Figure 6.2 Symbols used to support behavioural expectations at group time

ACTIVITY 7

Making continuous provision inclusive

- *Why is it important that the books on offer to children represent the diversity in society? In what ways can this be considered inclusive practice?*

- *In what ways is having a toy and story sack library inclusive practice?*

- *Investigate how the use of Makaton signs alongside speech supports children's language and communication development? Consider all children: children who are making the expected progress with their language and communication and children who need support. Why is it important to have these systems in place?*

- *Why is it important to organise space in settings to ensure everyone can move round easily and that there are opportunities for activities in different places and spaces, for example, on table tops, on the floor, indoors and outdoors?*

Providing additional support to children

It is a legal requirement for OFSTED-registered settings and schools to ensure that they meet the needs of children who require additional support with their learning and development. The Special Educational Needs Code of Practice (2001) provides advice and guidance on how to carry out statutory duties to identify, assess and make provision for children who have special educational needs.

The Code of Practice defines Special Educational Needs as follows:

Children have special educational needs if they have a learning difficulty which calls for special educational provision to be made for them.

Children have a *learning difficulty* if they:

- have significantly greater difficulty in learning than the majority of children of the same age;

- have a disability that prevents or hinders them from making use of educational facilities of a kind generally provided for children of the same age in schools within the area of the local authority;

- are under compulsory school age and fall within the definition above or would do so if special provision were not made for them.

Children must not be regarded as having a learning difficulty solely because that language or form of language of their home is different from the language in which they will be taught.

Special educational provision means:

- for children age two or over, educational provision which is additional to, or otherwise different from, the educational provision made generally for children of their age in schools maintained by the local authority;

- for children under age two, educational provision of any kind.

For most children it is expected that their needs will be met within their local childcare setting and their local school. This process is often referred to as inclusion; the expectation that all local children will attend their local school or early years setting. Schools and early years settings are expected, within reason and legal requirements, to organise their provision and resources in ways that enable all children and families to access the provision. This includes a commitment by staff to develop their knowledge and professional skills to understand the ways in which provision can be made inclusive and, when appropriate, how to meet the needs of children in their setting who have additional or special educational needs.

Clearly for some children who have very complex needs and require expert care and specialist teaching, their needs may have to be met in specialist units, schools or settings. These schools and settings often have expertise in supporting the learning and development of children with complex needs. For many children with complex needs, provision is set up so that they spend time in specialist schools or units and time in mainstream schools and settings with staff from the specialist provision working with staff in the mainstream setting to develop their knowledge and skills to support the inclusion of individual children. This specialist provision is necessary to ensure appropriate provision for some children with complex needs. However, for most children the fundamental principle is that their needs should be met within local provision alongside their peers and siblings.

CASE STUDY

Michael is four years old and has a diagnosis of autistic spectrum disorder. He attends a mainstream school. He has some spoken language although his pronunciation is not always clear. He is helped by photo and/or symbolic representation. To support Michael's transition into school the staff put in place a number of things before he started.

- *They made a book of photographs (with symbols) of all the places in the nursery that Michael would use in a day, for example, where he would put his coat, the toilets and indoor and outdoor play areas.*

- *They made a book of photographs (with symbols) of the daily routine in the nursery.*

- *They made a chart of photographs of all the staff that Michael would come across at nursery.*

- *The SENCO and his keyworker visited Michael at home to find out about the ways that Michael's family meet his needs and to share the books and charts with Michael and his family. They left the books and charts at Michael's home so that he could look at them with his mum.*

Together Michael's mum, his keyworker, the SENCO and the specialist teacher from the local authority agreed how they would support Michael in the setting.

- *Michael took his favourite soft toy into Nursery each day to ease the transition between home and nursery.*

- *The staff created a fan of photographs (with symbols) of the places he would be going and the people he would meet in nursery so that they could carry this with them as a visual aid to support Michael's understanding of what was happening.*

- *The staff also used objects of reference to support Michael's understanding of expectations and routines; for example, a book to show him that it was storytime, a cup to show him that it was snack time, a bag to show him it was time to go home.*

- *They taught Michael some phrases that he could learn and use, for example, to ask for help or ask someone to play.*

- *The staff agreed to use clear unambiguous language when interacting with Michael.*

The staff were able to create the photograph charts, books and fan and understood the need to use objects of reference to support Michael's understanding of routines and expectations. However, they were unsure about what the use of clear unambiguous language meant in their daily interactions, and how best to teach Michael phrases that he

continued

CASE STUDY *continued*

could use when in nursery. They sought advice from the specialist teacher who was work-ing with Michael. She came into the nursery and worked alongside the staff modelling the best way to interact with Michael and how to encourage him to use words and phrases to meet his needs.

This support enabled Michael to settle into nursery well. His progress and well-being and the support offered are monitored carefully by the staff to ensure that his needs continue to be met in the nursery.

Meeting children's needs in mainstream provision: assessing children's needs and providing support

When there are concerns about a child's developmental progress, procedures for observing and assessing their needs must be followed as set down in the Special Educational Needs Code of Practice (2001). Each setting is required to have a SENCO (Special Educational Needs Co-ordinator). This person is responsible for ensuring that children who require additional support are identified and the appropriate steps are taken to meet their needs.

Some children will come into settings with their needs already identified and support ser-vices in place. This might be speech therapists, paediatricians, social workers or teachers of the deaf – depending upon the child's needs. The setting will be expected to work along-side these professionals to support the child's needs.

Other children will be identified within settings. It is the responsibility of all Early Years practitioners to be aware of children's learning and development and to identify children about whom they have concerns. Settings are required to have a key person system in place and it is expected that one of the roles of the key person is to observe, assess and monitor each of their children's developmental progress. If they have concerns about a child they must let the SENCO know. At this stage parents must be notified that the set-ting has concerns about their child. There is a requirement to inform parents at each stage of any assessment process unless there are safeguarding concerns, in which case there are other procedures. The SENCO can then work with the parents and practitioners to iden-tify what the child's needs are. Once the child's needs have been identified, the staff and SENCO must put in place additional support to meet these needs in the setting. This may be enhancing existing provision, it may be additional activities, or it may be more indi-vidual focused time with a staff member. The agreed plan for support is often written down as an Individual Education Plan (IEP). This identifies clear targets for the child which everyone can work towards. The most effective practice is when settings and parents work together and the additional support is put in place at home and in the setting. This stage of support is called Early Years Action in pre-school settings and School Action in schools.

If, after additional support has been put in place, staff and parents continue to have con-cerns about a child's development, the next stage is to involve outside agencies. These are other professionals who can further support the child's learning and development accord-ing to need. A range of services for children are available through the local authority, health services and voluntary sector. This stage is called Early Years Action Plus or School Action Plus.

If it is then agreed that the child's needs are still not being met, there is a formal assessment process which can result in the child having a statement of special educational needs. This statement places a legal duty upon the local authority to make the necessary provision for meeting the child's needs. These stages are called Statutory Assessment and Statementing.

This approach to identifying and meeting children's needs is called a 'graduated approach,' as each step gradually increases the level and breadth of support until the child's needs are met. See Table 6.2.

Meeting children's needs: A graduated approach	
Early Years Action	The SENCO, in consultation with key person and parents: includes the child's name on the SEN register and records this in the child's file, assesses the child's needs, ensures provision is appropriately differentiated to meet the child's needs, prepares an IEP if appropriate and reviews progress regularly
Early Years Action Plus	The SENCO requests external and specialist input: requests specialist assessments and advice, develops new strategies in partnerships with other agencies, informs parents of this process and reviews progress regularly
Statutory Assessment	The Local Authority makes a multi-disciplinary assessment of the child's needs
Statement of Special Educational Needs	A statement of special educational needs is written indicating the child's needs and the recommended provision to meet these needs

Table 6.2 Meeting children's needs: a graduated approach

Meeting all children's learning and development needs within The Early Years Foundation Stage

The approach within the EYFS recognises the impact that external factors can have on children's learning and development, and the role that an inclusive approach to provision has in challenging disadvantage and discrimination. The issue of provision for all children is a thread running through the EYFS.

- One of the four guiding principles that should shape practice in Early Years settings states that *children develop and learn in different ways and at different rates. The framework covers the education and care of all children in early years provision, including children with special educational needs and disabilities* (DFE, 2012, p.3).

- The statutory framework states that *providers must have and implement a policy, and procedures, to promote equality of opportunity, including support for children who are disabled or have special educational needs. The policy should cover: how the individual needs of all children will be met (including how those children who are disabled or have special educational needs, will be included, valued and supported, and how reasonable adjustments will be made for them); the name of the SENCO; arrangements for reviewing, monitoring and evaluating the effectiveness of inclusive practices that promote and value diversity and difference; how inappropriate attitudes and practices will be challenged; and how provision will encourage children to value and respect others* (DFE, 2012, p.26).

- The aims of the EYFS progress check at age two include that practitioners should note areas where children are progressing well and identify any areas where progress is less than expected so that they can take action to address developmental concerns, including working with other professionals where appropriate.

It is therefore important that early years practitioners are well informed about the factors that can affect children's learning and development, and, know how to work with children, and with other agencies, to, as far as possible, ameliorate these affects and to promote positive attitudes towards others and towards difference.

CHAPTER SUMMARY

In this chapter we have explored the different factors that affect children's learning and development. We have seen that the impact of different factors causes some children's development to fall outside of expected developmental parameters. This may mean that a child's development falls below or exceeds developmental expectations, or, that their profile of development is atypical. The importance of supporting all children's learning and development needs is explored as a human and disability rights issue. The history of inclusion for children with special educational needs is briefly described and the development and processes of the current, inclusive approach is explored, including the statutory graduated response to identifying and responding to children's needs. The role of the Early Years practitioners in providing an inclusive learning environment, that meets the learning and development needs of all children, is outlined.

FURTHER READING

Baldock, P (2010) *Understanding cultural diversity in the early years.* London: Sage.

Bissex, G (1980) *GNYS AT WORK. A child learns to read and write.* Cambridge, MA: Harvard University Press.

Bowlby, J (1953) *Child care and the growth of love.* Harmondsworth: Penguin.

Casey, T (2010) *Inclusive play.* London: Sage.

DCSF (2009) *Deprivation and education.* DCSF. **https://www.education.gov.uk/publications/ standard/publicationDetail/Page1/DCSF-RTP-09-01**

DFE (2012) *Statutory Framework for the Early Years Foundation Stage.* DFE. **https://www.education. gov.uk/publications/standard/publicationDetail/Page1/DFE-00023-2012**

DFES (2001) *Special Education Needs Code of Practice.* DFES. **https://www.education.gov.uk/ publications/standard/publicationDetail/Page1/DFES%200581%202001**

Dukes, C and Smith, M (2006) *A practical guide to pre-school inclusion.* London: Paul Chapman Publishing.

Farrell, P and Ainscow, M (2002) *Making special education inclusive.* London: David Fulton Publishers.

Feinstein (2003) in DCSF (2009) Deprivation and education. DCSF. **https://www.education.gov.uk/ publications/standard/publicationDetail/Page1/DCSF-RTP-09-01**

Griffin, J and Tyrrell, I (1997) *Human givens. A new approach to emotional health and clear thinking.* East Sussex: HG Publishing. **www.humangivens.com/home.php**

Griffin, J and Tyrrell, I (2007) *An idea in practice. Using the human givens approach.* East Sussex: HG Publishing. **www.humangivens.com/home.php**

Guldberg, H (2009) *Reclaiming childhood. Freedom and play in an age of fear.* London: Routledge.

Hart, B and Risley, T (1995) *Meaningful differences in the everyday experience of young American children.* London: Paul H. Brookes Publishing.

Hirsch (2007) in DCSF (2009) *Deprivation and education.* DCSF. **https://www.education.gov.uk/publications/standard/publicationDetail/Page1/DCSF-RTP-09-01**

Hobbs (2003) in DCSF (2009) *Deprivation and education.* DCSF. **https://www.education.gov.uk/publications/standard/publicationDetail/Page1/DCSF-RTP-09-01**

Kahn, T and Young, N (2007) *Embracing equality. Promoting equality and inclusion in the Early Years.* London: Pre-School Learning Alliance.

Nutbrown, K and Clough, P (2006) *Inclusion in the early years.* London: Sage.

Reay (2006) in DCSF (2009) *Deprivation and education.* DCSF. **https://www.education.gov.uk/publications/standard/publicationDetail/Page1/DCSF-RTP-09-01**

Skelton, C, Francis, B and Valkanova, Y (2007) *Breaking down the stereotypes. Gender and achievement in schools.* Equal Opportunities Commission Working paper number 59 **www.equalityhumanrights.com/en/publicationsandresources/gender/pages/research.aspx**

Social Exclusion Task Force (2008) in DCSF (2009) *Deprivation and education.* DCSF. **https://www.education.gov.uk/publications/standard/publicationDetail/Page1/DCSF-RTP-09-01**

Sylva, K, Meluish, E, Sammons, P, Siraj-Blatchford, I and Taggart, B (2004) *The effective provision of pre-school education (EPPE) project. Findings from pre-school to the end of Key Stage 1.* SureStart. **www.education.gov.uk/publications/standard/publicationDetail/Page1/DfES/1081/2004**

Washbrook, E and Waldfogel, J (2010) *Low income and early cognitive development in the UK.* The Sutton Trust. **www.suttontrust.com/annualreports.asp**

WEBSITES

www.selfdirection.org/dat/training?cmd=guest&p=%2Fcourse01%2Fwelcome.html
An online exploration of social and medical models of disability

www.cabinetoffice.gov.uk/social_exclusion_task_force Social Exclusion Task Force

www.CSIE.org.uk Centre for Studies on Inclusion

www.cpag.org.uk Child Poverty Action Group (CPAG)

www.cls.ioe.ac.uk Centre for Longitudinal Studies. Houses three renowned cohort studies: National Child Development Study; British Cohort Study; Millennium Cohort Study.

Section 3

Applying child development in practice

7 Supporting children's learning and development

This chapter will enable you to understand:

- how young children learn and develop;
- why the development of language is vital to young children's learning;
- the pedagogical practices that best support young children's learning and development;
- why working in partnership with parents is the best way to support young children's learning.

Introduction

It is important that early years practitioners know how young children learn and develop and how to support this effectively. Alongside an understanding of expected development progress practitioners need to know how best to create an environment that supports learning and be skilled in the pedagogical practices that support children's learning. Practitioners need to be able to sensitively adapt what they do and what they provide to meet the needs of the children.

How do young children learn?

Young children learn and develop through being active in the world around them. They explore, investigate, observe and experience their world through all their senses. Children learn through talk and through listening. Talk and listening enable children to develop language that gives them a powerful tool for understanding, thinking and communicating. Children learn best in a context of warm, secure and safe relationships.

This need for active, exploratory, experiential, interactive learning is best met through play. It is widely acknowledged that play is a vital medium for young children's learning (Moyles, 2005). This is recognised in the Early Years Foundation Stage (DFE, 2012, p.6), which states that *each area of learning and development must be implemented through planned purposeful play... play is essential for children's development*. Play allows young children to learn actively.

- Play is enjoyable.

- Play is engaging and motivating.

- Play is interactive and experiential.

- Play allows children to explore and consolidate their current learning.

- Play provides challenge to move children's learning forward.

- Play cannot be wrong; it enables children to explore and investigate their world in a safe and secure way.

- Play allows for a creative and playful approach to learning and development.

- Play enables children to transform their knowledge and understanding through active direct experience in their world.

- Play enables children to engage in concrete experiences that support the early stages of symbolic representation and later abstract thought.

Our understanding of how young children learn and develop is underpinned by developmental theory. There are a number of influential theorists in Early Years whose work articulates why an active, play-based, exploratory and interactive learning environment will best support the learning and development needs of young children. Early Years practitioners need to be well informed about learning theory to enable them to select, integrate and apply this knowledge in their provision and interaction to best support children's learning and development.

Jean Piaget (1896–1980)

The work of Jean Piaget is widely recognised as having a significant impact on our current understanding of how children learn. He developed the hypothesis that children think in different ways to adults. His research showed that children gather and process information in ways that are unique to childhood. Some of his findings have been questioned but the basis of his research, that children are not just 'little adults' in the way they think, remains a fundamental part of our understandings of early childhood development.

Piaget outlined a series of stages that, amongst other things, describe how children gather and process information. These stages form the basis of Piaget's understanding of how young children think and learn.

THEORY FOCUS

Piaget's stages of development

Sensory motor stage 0–2 years

- Children gather information predominantly through their senses of sight and touch.

- Children process information imagistically (as images).

- Children have a tendency to be egocentric – to see the world from their own viewpoint.

- Children tend to use trial and error as their main tool of discovery.

Children in this age range have limited language ability; therefore, senses other than hearing are predominant in their learning. Sight and touch are vital senses in enabling a child to gather information in their environment. This learning is then processed as images,

---

similar to, but more sophisticated than pictures or photographs. This processing system is inflexible and has limited use. For example, how would you store the concept of freedom in this way? Children therefore need to develop language. It is immediately obvious that there is an important relationship between language, thinking and learning.

Pre-operational stage 2–7 years

This stage is divided into:

- pre-conceptual stage 2–4;

- intuitive stage 5–7.

Throughout this stage children develop language and increasingly use it to think and communicate. Language is a complex system of representation for both thinking and communicating. Again, the link between language and thinking and communicating is clear; language is vital in children's learning.

Pre-conceptual stage 2–4

- Children continue to gather information predominantly through sight and touch but language becomes increasingly important.

- Initially children process information imagistically (through images). However, it gradually becomes mediated by thought processes as children's language develops. Thoughts are still quite straightforward and dependent upon immediate perceptions of their environment.

- Children still tend to be egocentric.

- Children believe that everything has consciousness, for example, dolls have feelings, tables are naughty. Piaget terms this animism.

- Children begin to play symbolically, to use one object to represent another, for example, bricks as food, a doll as a baby, a stick as a sword.

Intuitive stage 5–7

- Hearing/listening gradually becomes the predominant sense for taking in information.

- Thought processes are increasingly mediated by language as it develops.

- Symbolic play continues and becomes more sophisticated as language develops.

- Children are still dependent upon immediate perceptions of their environment and find abstract thought more difficult.

Piaget and the development of concepts

Once a child has developed sufficient language skills, learning can be processed as concepts. Concepts is the way in which learning is organised cognitively, for example, a range of meanings can be recalled by the words 'high' 'love' 'strong' or 'achievement'.

Concepts range from the straightforward such as 'colour' or 'wet,' to the more complex and abstract such as 'freedom' or 'justice'. Young children are at the stage of developing, adapting and refining concepts. Concepts are developed through meaningful interaction with the environment and with others, adults and children.

Piaget describes how children acquire concepts – Piaget uses the term 'schemas' – through the processes of assimilation and accommodation, equilibrium and disequilibrium.

- Assimilation – the way in which children take in information through their experiences.

- Accommodation – the way in which children adapt existing information to accommodate new experiences into existing concepts or schemas.

- Disequilibrium – when a child comes across a new experience that requires assimilation or accommodation.

- Equilibrium – when a child has successfully assimilated and accommodated new learning into a concept and has reached a position of stasis.

ACTIVITY 1

Think of your understanding of the concept of love.

- *Create a mind map of your concept of love.*

- *Look carefully at your mind map. Notice all the different connections and interpretations and meanings you have within that concept.*

- *Consider how you developed these understandings. Who and what has been significant in the development of this concept?*

- *Compare your mind map with another person's mind map.*

- *What are the similarities?*

- *What are the differences?*

- *Why do you think that your concepts of love have similarities and differences?*

Piaget's work can be seen to provide a rationale for play as an effective way for children to learn and develop. Play allows children to learn in a multi-sensory way. It provides the opportunity for children to explore their world in a way that is meaningful for them to adapt and refine concepts. Play allows children to engage in concrete experiences and to use these experiences in concert with their developing language to move towards more abstract thinking. Repetition and differentiation within activities is possible so there is scope for developing more complex concepts through the processes of assimilation and accommodation.

Critiques of Piaget's work
Piaget's work has remained important in early years. However, further research has questioned some of the tenets of Piaget's work. In the 1970s Margaret Donaldson challenged a number of Piaget's findings. She based this on a critique of the ways in which Piaget

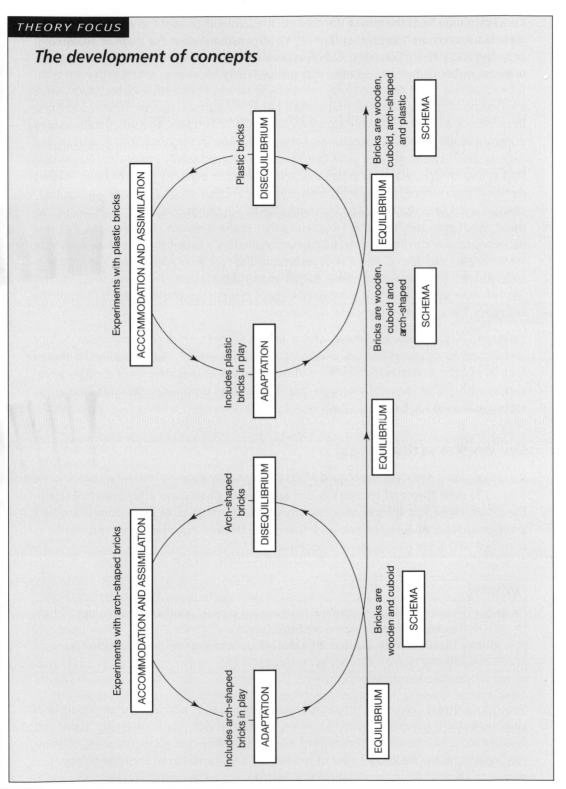

THEORY FOCUS

The development of concepts

Figure 7.1 Example of a child developing a schema for bricks
Adapted from Neaum and Tallack (1997)

asked questions in experimental conditions. She contends that there was a tendency to try and catch children out rather than try to offer opportunities for them to show what they were capable of. Donaldson (1978) argued that if children were questioned in a naturalistic, rather than experimental, setting they would be able to better articulate what they knew and could do. Therefore, some of the assumptions within Piaget's work were a reflection of the ways in which he worked rather than a reflection of children's abilities. Donaldson's work was followed up by a number of researchers and other studies were done to challenge Piaget's conclusions. For example, Martin Hughes (1978, in Neaum and Tallack, 1997) challenged the view that children were necessarily egocentric. Piaget said that young children were not capable of seeing another person's point of view. Hughes demonstrated experimentally that, after some instruction about the experimental task, children aged between three and five were able to see things other than their own viewpoint. What emerged from this work, and other similar research, was the idea that it is necessary to give children optimal help in understanding a task if they are to demonstrate what they are capable of. This means presenting the task in as meaningful a way as possible and using language and concepts that young children are likely to understand. This has led some people to adopt a modified view of Piaget's work; others do not accept the criticisms. These are ongoing academic debates.

However, despite these challenges and criticisms Piaget's work remains central to our understanding of young children's learning and development. Piaget outlined a theory that, in practice, understands learning and development as requiring direct concrete experiences with a wide range of materials and activities and progression towards a linguistic representation of the world.

Lev Vygotsky (1896–1934)

Vygotsky's ideas have had a profound effect on our understanding of how young children learn. The main theme of his work is that social interaction plays a fundamental role in the development of cognition. Vygotsky argued that learning takes place alongside others through collaborative interaction and dialogue. Effective, engaged social interaction is therefore vital in the development of cognitive skill.

Definition	
Cognition	The mental processes involved in gaining knowledge and comprehension, including thinking, knowing, remembering, judging, and problem solving
	These are higher-level functions of the brain and involve language, imagination, perception and planning

Vygotsky's theory clearly has implications for the ways in which we understand how children learn. It requires a learning context in which children and adults are active and involved in social interaction. This marked a significant shift in our understanding of learning, away from the traditional view of learning as a transmission of knowledge from one person to another, to an understanding of learning as a collaborative and reciprocal social process. In Vygotsky's theory learning takes place when the interaction is purposeful and meaningful for the learner. This means that interaction needs to be based on a good understanding of both the learners' current level of understanding and their next steps in learning. Vygotsky developed the idea of a 'zone of proximal development' to explain this process. He suggested that a child has two stages of development: their present level of development; and the next step that can, as yet, only be achieved with a more knowledge-able others' help. The more knowledgeable other (often an adult) needs to support the child's learning until they can achieve the next step alone.

Vygotsky's Zone of Proximal Development (ZPD)

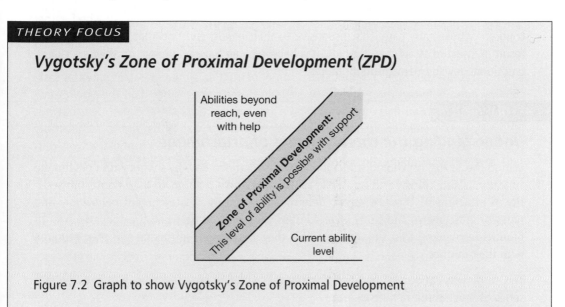

Figure 7.2 Graph to show Vygotsky's Zone of Proximal Development

This understanding of learning and development is well established within early years pedagogical practice. Vygotskian theory supports dynamic interaction during play and focuses on the importance of knowing what a child can do as the starting point for focused interaction to support the next stage of their learning and development. This way of understanding children's learning necessitates a very good understanding of children's development and of effective interactive processes that support learning and development.

John Bowlby (1907–1990)

Attachment theory

The work of John Bowlby, and later with Mary Ainsworth, on attachment theory offers an understanding of why children learn best within the context of warm, safe and secure relationships.

Attachment is an emotional bond to another person. It emerges from the special emotional relationship that involves an exchange of comfort, care, and pleasure between a young child and their parent or another significant carer. Attachment theory was developed by John Bowlby. Bowlby held the view that early experiences in childhood have an important influence on later development. Our early attachment style, he argues, is established in childhood through our earliest relationships and have an impact throughout our lives. The central tenet of attachment theory is that mothers who are available and responsive to their baby's needs establish a sense of security. The baby learns that the mother is dependable, which creates a secure base for the child to explore the world. It is though that through this warm responsive care children create an internal working model of security and support that enables them to develop a positive self-image and an expectation of positive responses from others. Although Bowlby's initial research stressed the role of mothers there is evidence to suggest that a bond of attachment can be formed with other carers who fulfil the role of offering warm, consistent, responsive care.

When children receive warm responsive care they are said to be securely attached. Other children, whose early care isn't responsive to their needs, can find that these experiences result in insecure attachments which, it is believed, can have an impact on their social and emotional development throughout life.

THEORY FOCUS

Understanding the characteristics of attachment

During the 1970s, psychologist Mary Ainsworth expanded Bowlby's work with her 'strange situation' study (Ainsworth and Bell, 1970). Ainsworth wanted to investigate the security of attachment. The aim was to determine the nature of attachment behaviours and types of attachment. The study involved observing children between the ages of 12 to 18 months responding to a situation in which they were briefly left alone and then reunited with their mother.

The study was conducted by observing the behaviour of parents/carers and children in a series of seven three-minute events.

1 Parent/carer and child are alone.

2 Stranger joins the parent and child.

3 Parent leaves the child and stranger alone.

4 Parent returns and the stranger leaves.

5 Parent leaves – the child is left on their own.

6 Stranger returns.

7 Parent returns and the stranger leaves.

The team was interested in observing aspects of the child's behaviour such as:

- separation anxiety when separated from the parent/carer;

- stranger anxiety when with the stranger;

- reaction when reunited with parent.

These observations revealed three distinct types of attachment: secure, insecure ambivalent and insecure avoidant.

Secure attachment

- Securely attached children exhibit minimal distress when separated from parent/carer. These children feel secure and able to depend on their adult carers. When the adult leaves, the child feels assured that the parent or carer will return.

- When frightened, securely attached children will seek comfort from carers. These children know their parent or carer will provide comfort and reassurance, so they are comfortable seeking them out in times of need.

Insecure resistant/ambivalent attachment

- Ambivalently attached children usually become very distressed when a parent leaves. Research suggests that ambivalent attachment is a result of poor maternal availability. These children cannot depend on their mother (or carer) to be there when the child is in need.

Insecure avoidant attachment

- Children with an avoidant attachment tend to avoid parents or carers. When offered a choice, these children will show no preference between a known carer and a complete stranger. Research has suggested that this attachment style might be a result of abusive or neglectful carers.

The methods used by Ainsworth and Bell have been criticised for a number of reasons. For example, the study only deals with the relationship with the mother and not other significant familial relationships; the children were put in an artificial experimental situation which may have influenced their responses; putting children in stressful situations for research purposes is unethical; a child may be displaying behaviours that are because of the current context of their lives, perhaps their mother had been ill, rather than an ongoing relational issue. Some of these criticisms have challenged some of the claims made regarding attachment.

However, despite these criticisms, the idea of secure and insecure attachments has had a profound effect upon our understanding of the importance of children's need for warm responsive parenting/care in their early life and has offered a way of understanding and interpreting the difficult behaviour of children who have suffered distress in their early life.

The importance of attachment

Having a secure bond of attachment to another person is regarded as a foundation for successful social and emotional development. It has been observed that children with secure attachments are more socially competent than those with insecure attachment. Social competence is associated with high self-esteem and empathy towards others. These traits make it easier for children to be liked and therefore to form and maintain familial relationships and friendships.

It is probable that social competence and good self-esteem flow from securely attached children's early exploratory impulses. Their secure attachments enable them to engage with the world with a sense of confidence, curiosity and enthusiasm precisely because they have a secure base to leave and return to, confident in the knowledge that it will be there when they return. The sense of security and support engendered by responsive care enables the child to develop a positive sense of self and positive expectations of their relationships with others. In contrast, children who have insecure attachments are more likely to display clingy, anxious behaviours in social situations which limits their interaction and engagement with the world.

Children with secure attachments are also known to show more co-operative behaviours with their parents. This may be as a result of their greater social competency. This behaviour has many beneficial effects. Children who are more co-operative towards their parents are more likely to listen and interact in a positive way, therefore enhancing their opportunities for further developing their social skills and other aspects of their learning. This creates a positive upward spiral; children are socially competent therefore they interact effectively in different situations and with different people, this means that they have opportunities to learn and develop their skills and knowledge in all areas of development, which means that they then have greater skill and knowledge in their interactions, and so it goes on. Unfortunately the opposite is often true for children who lack social skills and competencies. Their chances for interacting appropriately and developing interactive skills that support learning and development are often very limited by their lack of social competency. Children can then get trapped in patterns of interaction, both at home and in settings and at school, that don't support their learning and development.

There is a growing amount of research that suggests that children who have experienced distress in early life that have resulted in insecure attachments can be helped through interventions with the child and/or the family. Interventions can be preventative and therapeutic (Broberg, 2000). This is skilled work. It requires assessment and intervention from professionals who understand the issues and the processes involved. These services can be accessed through a school or setting SENCO, through health services, and through children's services in children's centres.

In line with the aims of Every Child Matters the best approach with children who are regarded as being at risk is a proactive one. In this approach people who work with children and families are alert to the possibilities of relational difficulties in families and offer support and guidance to parents. The aim is to enable parents to respond to their children in warm and responsive ways that are likely to lead to the creation of secure bonds of attachment. It is from a starting point of these warm, safe and secure relationships that children develop and learn best.

The role of the adult in promoting positive emotional and social development

- From the earliest age demonstrate love and offer affection as well as meeting their developmental needs
- Give appropriate praise for effort, more than achievement
- Demonstrate that you value what they do and produce
- Explain why rules exist and why children should do what you are asking them to do. Where possible use 'do' rather than 'don't' and emphasise what you want the child to do rather than what is not acceptable. When children misbehave explain to them why it is wrong.
- Stay on the child's side – assume that they mean to do right not wrong
- Provide babies opportunities to explore the world through all five senses
- Give children activities that are a manageable challenge. Remember that children need time alone as well as with others and involved in activities
- Provide opportunities for role play – to explore other roles and experiences
- Encourage children to use language to express their own feelings and thoughts, and how they think others feel
- Be interested in what the child is saying – give the child attention and listen to what they say. Do not laugh at a child's response when it is not intended to be funny
- Don't use put-downs or sarcasm – they have a negative impact on children's sense of self
- Encourage children to be self-dependent and responsible
- Encourage children to follow through activities and tasks to completion
- Provide children with their own things which they know belong to them
- Provide good flexible role models with regard to gender, disability and ethnicity
- Encourage children to value their own cultural background

Table 7.1 Promoting positive emotional and social development

The importance of language in young children's learning

The development and use of speech, language and communication are at the heart of young children's learning (DCSF, 2008, p.8). Learning theory supports this view; that the development of language is fundamental to learning. Language is a learned skill that we require to think and to communicate. Therefore, the more effective children's language learning, the more effective children's language for communication and language for thinking are likely to be. This in turn will support their learning and development across all areas of development throughout their life.

ACTIVITY 2

As you work through this activity be aware of your thought processes.

1   *Imagine a car, imagine a table, imagine a shoe.*

    How did you recall these things? What was 'in your head?'

2   *Imagine a home, imagine friendship, imagine beauty.*

    How did you recall these things? How much was imagistically? How much language based?

3   *Imagine justice, imagine tolerance, imagine freedom.*

---

continued

ACTIVITY *continued*

How did you recall these things? How much was imagistically? How much language based?

- *Look carefully at these three sections. What is the difference between the use of images and language as a tool for thinking in these three instances?*

- *What are the implications of this for children's development of language for learning?*

- *What does this suggest about how the quality of a child's language affects their learning?*

There is evidence to suggest that we are born with the potential to develop language, for example, Noam Chomsky's work on the language acquisition device, but we need to be exposed to language and have opportunities to use language in meaningful contexts to learn and develop effective language and communication skills. This is important. Language is a learned skill. Early Years practitioners therefore need to know how to best support children's language development to enable them to develop and learn.

THEORY FOCUS

Noam Chomsky: Language Acquisition Device (LAD)

Noam Chomsky (in Aitchison, 2008) worked in the field of psycholinguistics. He opposed the traditional learning theory understanding of language learning as stimulus–response and instead proposed that linguistic knowledge and understanding were the result of a universal innate ability termed a 'language acquisition device' – that we are born with the building blocks of language.

One of the important underpinning reasons for this proposition is the ease with which we all learn our first language. He observed two important facets of young children's language learning.

1 Young children learn to understand grammatically correct language despite the fact that the spoken language they hear is often not grammatically correct, for example, we use half sentences, incorrect words, incorrect grammatical formulations, interrupt and change what we are saying, use interjections. Children acquire language much quicker than other abilities, and, almost all children acquire and can correctly use very complex language.

Read these two sentences. One of them 'makes sense' – we hear it as 'correct' – even though it is nonsense.

Colourless green ideas sleep furiously.

Ideas furiously green colourless sheep.

Not many of us could explain the grammatical process in these sentences but we can distinguish between them quite easily. Chomsky argues that we have an inherent ability to recognise underlying syntactical relationships in a sentence.

2 Children do not just copy the language that they hear. They appear to understand the underlying rules and apply them, despite never having heard that form of the language. This is most noticeable in mistakes that young children make.

Read these two sentences that young children may say.

I runned across the road.

I taked a picture of you.

- What mistake is being made?

- What grammatical structure are they applying incorrectly?

Chomsky argues that to make these apparent mistakes of applying regular grammatical rules to exceptions demonstrates the child's implicit understanding of the deep logical structure of language. They are never likely to hear anyone using this form of the verb but some children apply the regular rule and generate this form of the language. This idea of generating new language is important. Children don't just learn phrases that they hear they are able to generate an infinite number and variety of new sentences.

Jerome Bruner (1915–) extended the work of Chomsky with his idea of a language acquisition support system (LASS) (Bruner, 1984). Bruner suggested that alongside the LAD there must be a LASS if a child is going to learn language effectively. The LASS consists of all the people around the child who engage in interaction that enables the child to acquire language knowledge and skill. For children who attend a nursery, early years practitioners are part of this language acquisition support system.

Creating spaces in settings to develop speaking and listening

Elizabeth Jarman (2007) has developed some interesting work on creating *communication-friendly* spaces in settings. It flows from observation of learning spaces for young children in other countries such as Denmark and Sweden. She argues that the space in a setting can be organised in ways that encourage children to talk and to listen and so support the development of their language and communication. Speaking and listening, she argues, are encouraged by creating *communication-friendly spaces* (Jarman, 2007) within settings. There are a number of features of these spaces.

- Lack of extraneous stimuli. Practitioners are encouraged to create a calm environment through the use of muted natural colours for displays and resources, uncluttered wall and table top displays and well organised, readily available resources.

- As much natural light as possible.

- Gentle lighting where lighting is needed, such as the use of fairy lights.

- Low levels of background noise.

- Creating enclosed 'den-like' areas inside and outside that provide spaces for children to go and talk and read and play.

- Creating spaces that are specifically for talking and listening, such as a story-telling chair.

ACTIVITY 3

Look at the list of features of communication-friendly spaces.

- *Compare these features with your experience of play spaces for young children for example, in nurseries, playgroups, in the home.*

- *What changes need to be made to these spaces to create places that encourage children to use and develop their language skills?*

- *Think about your own work and home environment. Which spaces are most conducive to being calm, interacting well and working effectively?*

- *How does this map to what Jarman is suggesting for spaces for children's learning?*

- *What is your view about Jarman's ideas?*

These spaces are one way of encouraging children to engage in speaking and listening in the setting. However, 'communication-friendly spaces' won't support children's language development in themselves; they will only have an impact on children's language development if children are engaged in play and talk with their peers and the practitioners. Children's language development requires that they have opportunities to use, practice, adapt and refine their language knowledge and skills.

Because the development of children's language and communication skills is closely linked to the quality of the interaction that they are involved in, it is important that all early years practitioners know the most effective ways in which to interact with children to encourage the development of language for communication and language for thinking.

Pedagogical practices that best support young children's learning and development

Pedagogy and pedagogical practice is the art or method of teaching. It is a term that is used to encompass the whole range of interactive practices that support young children's learning. Early years has a strong recognisable pedagogical tradition that is different to teaching in schools. It is easily recognisable if you go into early years settings. Early years pedagogical practice involves supporting children's learning through play in ways that are responsive to children's interests and motivations. It involves a fluidity in the pace and timing of the experiences and interactions, and a commitment to being predominantly child-led. So what exactly is happening in the interactions? How is children's learning best supported in this learning environment? What are the most effective ways to interact with young children?

The REPEY study is a study of the most effective pedagogical strategies used at Foundation Stage level to support the development of young children's skills, knowledge and attitudes (Siraj-Blatchford et al., 2002). They found that there were a number of observable pedagogical practices evident in effective settings. This included: adult–child interactions; the way learning was monitored and how staff used this information; and how settings engaged in partnerships with parents.

The best learning takes place when children are motivated and involved (Siraj-Blatchford et al., 2002). It is assumed that the same is true of adults and so the most effective combination for learning is when:

- both the adult and the child are motivated and involved in the learning;

- interaction is collaborative and instructive;

- sustained shared thinking takes place (see definition).

Definition	
Sustained shared thinking	An episode in which two individuals work together in an intellectual way to solve a problem, clarify a concept, evaluate activities, extend a narrative, etc. Both parties must contribute to the thinking and it must develop and extend (Siraj-Blatchford et al., 2002, p.8)

Children also learn best when practitioners' interactions are at an appropriate developmental level. This means that practitioners need to monitor exactly what the children know and can do, and be aware of what comes next in children's learning and development so that they can match their interaction and teaching to the child's developmental needs. Effective pedagogical practice is to use observation to evaluate what learning is happening in order to understand what a child knows and can do, and to inform what happens next. This process of observation enables practitioners to offer formative feedback during activities. Formative feedback is feedback that is carried out during an activity and offers an evaluation of what learning is taking place, and, support and guidance on ways to develop the activity or experience to enhance the child's learning and development.

Finally, good developmental outcomes are best supported when parents provide a rich home learning environment. The role of settings is important in this. The REPEY study (Siraj-Blatchford et al., 2002) found that the best outcomes for children happen when settings support the ability of parents to provide a good home learning environment and don't just focus on meeting the adults' needs. This supports the view that what is important for young children's learning and development is not who parents are, but what they do.

Interaction to support children's learning and development

Other research that looked at the interactive processes of staff in a successful Nursery school found similar patterns of interaction that best supported children's learning and development (Neaum, 2005). One of the defining characteristics of positive interaction is playfulness; interaction in which practitioners clearly enjoy the processes of being engaged with the children in their learning. During activities practitioners need to be alive and sensitive to children's interests and engagement so that the direction, the pace and the timing of the activity are worked out together. This means that both the practitioners and children contribute to the understanding of the activity or experience; they construct their understandings together.

Positive interaction requires a range of interactive strategies that are used appropriately to support children's learning and development. There are many that can be used and are developmentally appropriate with young children, for example:

- discussion;
- pondering;
- questioning;
- modelling;
- direct teaching;
- the introduction of new vocabulary, as appropriate and in context.

Two other ways of interacting that have been shown to successfully support children's learning and development (Neaum, 2005) are the following.

- *Teachable moments*. These are moments that a child is particularly disposed to learn something. These moments arise during play and these opportunities can be used to move the child's learning forward. This teaching is done in a play-based context and requires a good understanding of children's learning and development, and of individual children, to judge the child's present level of understanding and what to teach next.

- *Commentary*. This is when a practitioner provides a verbal commentary on what is happening. Commentary offers the child a framework for their activity. It models use of language for communicating and language for thinking in a clear, direct context.

Commentary can be done in a number of ways, such as:

- providing a running commentary on what the child is doing – articulating the observable processes within the activity or experience;
- reflecting back the child's learning and making links between what the child is learning now and prior learning;
- practitioners providing a commentary of their own thoughts, ideas and questions as they engage in the activity alongside the child.

These ways of interaction between practitioners and children have many benefits for children's learning and development. It enables them to engage in sustained shared thinking. It is creative, enjoyable and intellectually challenging. The interaction is individually focused and so starts from each child's needs and abilities. It supports language for communication and language for thinking, and, it achieves all of this in a learning context that is fluid, open-ended and experiential.

Partnerships with parents

All the evidence suggests that a child's learning and development are enhanced when settings, early years practitioner's and parents work together. Working with parents as partners is one of the aims of the EYFS (DFE, 2012). It recognises that the best foundation for future progress is when there is partnership working between practitioners and parents. The importance of this partnership is a thread throughout the EYFS (DFE, 2012), for example, the requirement to involve parents in the assessment, and discuss the outcomes, of the two-year-old check.

The EPPE study (Sylva et al., 2003) concluded that what parents and carers do at home can make a big difference to their child's learning and development. In their assessments of the home learning environment they concluded that activities such as reading to children, teaching songs and nursery rhymes, painting and drawing, teaching them letters and numbers, taking them on visits and creating regular opportunities for them to play in the home with friends were all associated with higher intellectual and social/behavioural scores. This means that schools and settings need to support all parents in acquiring these skills. This is often achieved through the provision of programmes or individual support which aim to equip parents with the knowledge and skills to support their children's learning at home. This is usually organised through children's centres for children under the age of five. Schools and settings also need to foster parents' knowledge and skill by ensuring that there is good communication between home and school. This communication enables parents to be aware of their child's progress in the setting, and ensures that parents can share their knowledge of the child's learning and development at home. Schools and settings also need to provide opportunities for parents to continue to develop necessary knowledge and skills to support their child's learning and development at home.

Questions and controversies

While there is clearly evidence of the positive effects of engaged and interested parenting on children's learning and development, and so working in partnership with parents is an important aspect of our current system, it is not without controversy. Within the context of the necessity of working with parents it is worth considering what partnership with parents really means. Partnership suggests a two-way, dynamic relationship in which both partners bring a range of knowledge and skills to a situation in order to understand an issue or solve a problem. Clearly, at times, this will be achieved. However, it is argued that there is often a gap between the expectations of partnership and the lived reality. Within the context of services for children questions are asked about the exact nature of parental support and partnership working; whether working in partnership with parents really is working in partnership. The concern flows from the perception that there is an inbuilt imbalance in the relationship between professionals and parents as parenting has increasingly become an area of professionalization and intervention. This is particularly acute where parents are perceived to be in need of support. It is argued that the interventions are not, in practice, a partnership approach but are in fact based on a particular understanding of what it means to be a 'good parent' and the aim is to encourage parents to adopt this style of parenting. So whilst this approach is part of the partnership-with-parents initiative it isn't, in practice, a partnership relationship and to call it such can be seen as disingenuous.

ACTIVITY 4

Collect some prospectuses for nurseries and schools.

- *Read through the information provided about teaching and learning and partnerships with parents in the setting.*

- *How does this information help parents to support their child's learning at home?*

- *In what ways can the parents/carers share their knowledge about the child's learning and development at home with the school or setting?*

Find out about parenting programmes, both national programmes (for example, PEAL, The incredible years – Webster-Stratton, Positive parenting) and local programmes in your area.

- *What are their reasons for the provision of parenting programmes?*

- *How do these programmes aim to support parents in understanding and fostering learning at home?*

- *What are the known benefits of providing parenting programmes?*

- *What questions still remain about the efficacy of such programmes?*

- *What questions arise from programmes that are based on a particular understanding of parenting and aim to encourage parents to adopt this pattern of parenting?*

C H A P T E R   S U M M A R Y

In this chapter we have looked at how to play is vital for young children's learning. The learning theories of Piaget and Vygotsky are outlined to support this pedagogical approach. The significance of a secure bond of attachment to learning and development is explored through the work of Bowlby and Ainsworth. The important link between language and learning is explained and effective strategies for interacting with children are described. The home learning environment and working in partnership with parents is highlighted as being significant in supporting children's learning and development.

FURTHER READING

Aitchison, J (2008) *The articulate mammal.* Abingdon: Routledge.

Ainsworth, M and Bell, S (1970) Attachment, exploration and separation. *Child Development,* 41(1).

Bowlby, J (1953) *Child care and the growth of love.* London: Penguin.

Bretherton, I (1992) The origins of attachment theory: John Bowlby and Mary Ainsworth. *Developmental Psychology,* 28: 759–775.
www.psychology.sunysb.edu/attachment/online/inge_origins.pdf

Broberg, AG (2000) A review of interventions in the parent-child relationship informed by attachment theory. *Acta Paediatrica,* 89: 37–42.

Bruner, J (1984) *Child's talk. Learning to use language*. Oxford. Oxford University Press

DFE (2012) *Statutory Framework for the Early Years Foundation Stage*. DFE. **https://www.education. gov.uk/publications/standard/publicationDetail/Page1/DFE-00023-2012**

DCSF (2008) *Inclusion development programme. Supporting children with speech, language and communication needs: guidance for practitioners in the Early Years Foundation Stage*. DCFS Nottingham 00215-20008BKT-EN.
http://webarchive.nationalarchives.gov.uk/20110202093118/http:/nationalstrategies. standards.dcsf.gov.uk/search/inclusion/results/nav:46335

Donaldson (1978) cited in Sutherland, P (1992) *Cognitive development today. Piaget and his critics*. London: Paul Chapman Press.

Empson, J, Nabuzoka, D and Hamilton, D (2004) *Atypical child development in context*. Basingstoke. Palgrave MacMillan.

Jarman, E (2007) *Communication friendly spaces. Improving speaking and listening skills in the Early Years Foundation Stage*. Nottingham: Basic Skills Agency.
www.basic-skills.co.uk info@elizabethjarman.co.uk

Moyles, J (2005) *The excellence of play*. Maidenhead: Open University Press.

Neaum, S (2005) *Literacy, pedagogy and the early years*. Unpublished thesis. University of Nottingham.

Neaum, S (2012) *Language and literacy for the early years*. London: Sage.

Neaum, S and Tallack, J (1997) *Good practice in implementing the pre-school curriculum*. Cheltenham: Stanley Thornes.

Piaget, J (2001) *The psychology of intelligence*. London: Routledge.

Pound, L and Hughes, C (2005) *How children learn. From Montessori to Vygotsky*. London: Step Forward Publishing.

Siraj-Blatchford, I, Sylva, K, Muttock, S, Gilden, R and Bell, D (2002) *Researching effective pedagogy in the early years (REPEY)*. Research Report RR356. DCFS.
www.dfes.gov.uk/research/data/uploadfiles/RR356.pdf

Sylva, K, Meluish, E, Sammons, P, Siraj-Blatchford, I, Taggart, B and Elliot, K (2003) *Effective Provision of Pre-School (EPPE) Project: findings from the pre-school period*.
http://eppe.ioe.ac.uk/eppe/eppefindings.htm

Vygotsky, L (1978) *Mind in society*. Cambridge, MA: Harvard University Press.

Vygotsky, L (1986) *Thought and language*. Cambridge, MA: MIT Press.

8 Observing and assessing children's learning and development

This chapter will enable you to understand:

- why we observe and assess children's learning;
- what we can observe and assess;
- different techniques for observing and assessing children's learning and development;
- the requirement for observation-based assessment in the Early Years Foundation Stage.

Introduction

Assessment is the way in which in our everyday practice, we observe children's learning, strive to understand it, and then put our understanding to good use.

(Drummond, 1993)

When we watch children, watch them carefully and sensitively, we see them learning. When we approach observation of children with an open mind we can observe the richness of their play and interaction.

Through observation and assessment we can become aware of what children know and can do and use this information to ensure that what we provide and how we interact is closely linked to their abilities and needs.

Observing and assessing children's learning can also enhance our own knowledge and understanding of how children develop and learn. Detailed, careful, attentive observation, followed by well-informed assessment, can show us how children make meaning in their world, how they use and develop their language to enable then to communicate with others and to think. We can learn how they develop and maintain relationships, and how they develop emotionally and morally. This dynamic approach to observation and assessment enables us to go beyond the idea of normative developmental expectations and outcomes measures and enables us to really see, and celebrate, children as individuals.

Why is it important to observe and assess children's learning and development?

We use observation all the time in our personal and professional lives. We are constantly aware of what is happening around us and, through assessments that we make of situations, we adjust and refine our behaviour accordingly. For example, in settings, practitioners will notice when children have fallen over, they will notice that children have run out of glue, they will observe and monitor what needs doing as children tidy up. These informal observations are vital to the smooth running of the setting. Practitioners will also observe and notice the professional practice of colleagues to enhance their own practice. This might be informally; you notice that a colleague is working with children in an effective way and you observe her work as a model of how to do things well. It can also be done formally as professional development. For example, when areas for professional development are identified through appraisal practitioners can use focused observation of colleagues' practice, alongside analytical discussion, to learn and develop their own knowledge and skill.

ACTIVITY **1**

Think of some examples from your personal and/or professional life when you have observed another person with interest and the intention to understand what is happening.

- *What did you do as you made your observation?*
- *What were you thinking as you made your observation?*
- *How did you come to a conclusion about what was happening and why?*
- *What were your thoughts about how you could change as a result of what you observed?*
- *How did you change?*
- *Did it work? What changes did you make that are now embedded in who you are?*
- *How did observation and assessment help you understand what was happening and what change you could make?*

Observation and assessment is an effective way to understand children's learning and development. Using observation in this way is good practice. Young children's learning is evident in their play and interaction. It is through our observation and analysis of what we observe that we begin to understand the ways in which children make meaning in their world, and we come to know what they know and can do.

Why observe?

We observe children's play for a number of reasons.

- To understand what individual children know and can do.
- To understand what individual children are interested in and how they learn best so that we can support their learning and development effectively.
- To support overall planning and provision.
- To match our approaches and interactive strategies to children's needs to best support their learning and development.
- To further develop our understanding of how children learn, linking theory with practice.

The very best starting point for teaching children is to start with what they know and can do. Practitioners can establish this through attentive observation of children during their play. Careful observation and assessment will demonstrate to us what knowledge, skills and aptitudes children currently have and therefore, what is needed to further support their learning and development.

An important part of understanding children's learning is to observe what they are interested in. Where do they play? What do they play? Who do they play with? Which activities or experiences or themes engage them? Interest is an excellent motivator for children. When children are engaged in an activity or experience that is absorbing they are more likely to learn. We can use the information we gather through observation to inform what we do and what we provide. This ensures that we reflect children's interests in what we provide. Another important question to ask is: how do children learn best? This will be different for different children. Children will have a preferred way to explore their world; it might be alongside other children or alongside an adult; it may be in group work or on their own; it might be by returning over and over again to an activity; it might be singularly focused on an activity; it might be working with the same schema through a variety of different activities and experiences. Through observation practitioners need to become aware of individual children's preferences and, as with all other aspects of observation, ensure that provision caters for the children's ways of learning.

Observation and assessment of children and their learning also inform overall provision. The best way to support children's learning and development is to ensure that provision for both planned and child-initiated learning is closely matched to the needs of the children; both to meet their current needs and interests and provision that enables them to engage in activities and experiences that extend their learning. Observation should inform this process through careful analysis of the children's needs and interests reflected in the provision.

Observation and assessment should also inform pedagogical approaches within settings and schools. When practitioners have a good understanding of what children know and can do and of their needs practitioners can adapt their interactive strategies to best support children's learning and development.

CASE STUDY

Alex had been attending Nursery for about six months. At the Nursery practitioner observations of children are discussed at team meetings with the aim of adapting and matching their provision to the needs of the children. Alex's key person went through her observations of Alex highlighting what she had observed, saying what her assessments of Alex were and asking the other practitioners for their views on Alex. Overall both informal and formal observations showed that Alex had settled well and appeared to engage with and enjoy most activities. He appeared to particularly enjoy painting and spend some time at this activity each day. However, Alex's key person highlighted the fact that a number of the observations showed that although Alex appeared to be part of the group and engage in many activities, for much of the time he was watching others play or playing on his own or choosing activities, like painting, that he could do on his own. The staff discussed these observations and agreed that Alex needed more opportunities to engage in play with other children, either as one-to-one or within a group. They agreed to adapt their pedagogical approach to support Alex's learning. Over the next week Alex's key person would play alongside Alex and encourage and model playing with other children. At the following week's meeting they would review what had happened and, if necessary, continue to adapt their approach to meet Alex's needs.

- *How did the observation inform the practitioner's pedagogical approach?*

- *In this situation what professional knowledge and understanding did the practitioners have to enable them to understand what they had observed?*

- *What did staff have to know about early years pedagogy to enable them to adapt their approach?*

Observing children's play and learning is an excellent way of enhancing professional knowledge. Children are endlessly surprising. If we limit our observation to collecting information to assess children against developmental norms and prescribed criteria we will miss so much of the richness of their play. Drummond (1993) articulates this well: *if we choose to see only those aspects of learning of which we approve, we will lose the opportunity to see more of the picture, to learn more about learning ... there is always more to learn and more to see*. By being attentive and open to actually seeing what children know and can do we can learn from them. We may make clearer connections between theory and practice; we may observe things that we need to think about and reflect upon in order to understand exactly what was happening; we may see things that confound our expectations about individual children and/or expected developmental progress and stages. All of this enhances our professional knowledge and skill and enables us to develop a more sophisticated understanding of young children's learning and development.

Assessing children's learning

There are different ways of approaching the assessment of children's learning. At times you will need to do focused and purposeful observations so that you can assess a particular area of a child's learning. At other times your observation will be open and fluid and you will assess what emerges from the observation. Both are valid ways of assessing children's learning. Some examples of what you may find out from observation are:

- what children enjoy and are interested in;

- friendships;

- identifying specific learning needs;

- following up something that you have noticed informally and want to find out more;

- well-being;

- what a child is capable of within a particular area of development – physical, intellectual, language, emotional, social;

- which schemas children are developing;

- starting points for intervention;

- what a child knows and can do which will establish a child's developmental progress/level;

- to get to know a child better – open-ended.

THEORY FOCUS

Schemas

Athey (2007) describes schemas as *patterns of behaviour and thinking in children that exist under the surface features of various contents, contexts and specific experiences.*

She goes on to discuss what this looks like in practice:

> *you may have noticed children who seem to enjoy carrying out similar actions in a variety of ways, for example, a child who insists putting things in boxes, covering things up with scarves and hiding in dens. All of these may be an enclosure schema. Or, a child who enjoys playing with things that go round and round-wheels cars and cogs, and whose paintings have a circular energy to them. This may be a child with a rotation schema.*

Observing, identifying and working with children's schemas is one way of starting from the child. Schemas that are evident in children's play are, according to Athey (2007), a reflection of children's learning preferences and intrinsic brain patterns.

The notion of schemas as a way of understanding the development of children's thinking arose from the Frobel Early Education Project. The project aimed, though close observation of young children, to:

- *identify developments in each child's thinking;*

- *describe the development of symbolic representation;*

- *identify curriculum content relevant to developing forms of thought.*

The most significant finding of the project was the ideas of schemas as a way of understanding children's thinking and learning.

Cathy Nutbrown has continued and extended Athey's work. In her text *Threads of Thinking* Nutbrown (1999) highlights that Athey discusses children's development (schemas) and argues that they can be identified in children's drawings and are represented in children's play, their thinking and their language (Table 8.1).

Examples of schemas observable in young children's activities/interests	
Schema	Observable activity/interest
Trajectory – vertical and horizontal	Bouncing balls Throwing and kicking Climbing and jumping Water play with pipes and gutters Playing with running water from a tap Marble runs Climbing steps
Rotation	Fascination with spinning machines i.e. washing machine Play with toys with wheels Fascination with keys Rolling and spinning Painting with large circular motion Circle games
Transporting	Filling and moving objects in trucks and bags Pushing other children in pushchairs and prams
Enveloping and containing space	Climbing into boxes Filling containers Covering themselves up Wrapping dollies and teddies Building dens Painting whole sheets of paper one colour Wrapping or covering items in craft activities
Connecting	Train tracks and trains Construction Junk modelling

Table 8.1 Observable children's schemas

Clearly, all areas of children's learning and development can be assessed through observation. What is important is that that you approach both observation and assessment with the intention of finding something out. It is all too easy to find ourselves using observation and assessment to prove what we think that we already know rather than really focusing on what we have seen and analysing it with an open mind.

Assessment of observations requires a good understanding of child development and learning theory. It is this knowledge that will be applied to the observation as you analyse and interpret what you have seen and heard. It also requires that you have a good understanding of different observation techniques and when and how to use them to best effect.

Observation techniques

Different observation techniques need to be used to elicit different information. It is important that the information that you gather in your observation is appropriate and sufficiently detailed to enable you to make accurate assessments of children's learning.

Selecting an appropriate observation technique to gather your information is an important part of this process.

Different techniques include:

- time sampling;

- tracking;

- checklists;

- target child;

- learning stories;

- documenting.

Time sampling involves completing a short narrative observation of a child at 10–15 minute intervals. This gives you quite a broad overview of the child in the setting. Assessment of the observation can focused across many areas, as appropriate. The same technique can be used for activities. An activity is observed every 10–15 minutes. Again, this offers abroad range of possibilities for assessment.

Tracking observations follow children's choices within the setting. These choices (including time children spent between activities and any time they spent observing others) and the time that the child spends there is recorded. You may also record who else was at the activity and briefly how the child engaged with the activity/experience. Again, this offers a broad view of the child in the setting and assessment can be focused on what you need to know.

Checklists are pre-determined lists that identify knowledge, skills or aptitudes. The purpose of observation is to ascertain whether a child can meet these criteria. These can be useful if you need to find out something particular and precise. However, generally checklists are not a sufficiently sophisticated enough way of capturing the richness of young children's learning.

Target child observations are ones in which you identify a particular child to observe. You may be looking at something in particular or a completing an open ended observation. In this observation the child is observed within the learning environment alongside other children. This gives the child the opportunity to demonstrate what they know and can do within their familiar environment alongside their peers. The activity that the child is involved in is briefly recorded narratively and then language and social interactions are recorded and coded to give an accurate account of what happened during the observation for analysis and interpretation.

Learning stories are a way of recording and presenting observations of children over time; building a narrative about their learning. They emerged from the work of Margaret Carr and is based in sociocultural theory. Carr (2001) articulates a way of recording children's learning that acknowledges the context of that learning. She called these learning stories. The idea is to create a narrative, a story, recorded as a series of episodes linked together that record what the child knows and can do, and, records what comes next. This is important. The purpose of recording children's learning in learning stories is to enhance their learning, to foreground what they can do as starting point for providing for their ongoing development, and to recognise the complexity of the context and process of learning. The idea of a learning story is interpreted in a number of ways in practice. Some settings have formatted their observation sheets to create narrative threads linked to next steps in learning. Others have adopted a portfolio approach, in which observations and examples of children's work are kept together to create a narrative of their progress in the setting. Assessment of children's learning takes place at each stage of recording of the learning story in the analysis of the observation to define the next steps.

THEORY FOCUS

Sociocultural theory

Sociocultural theory is a belief that higher-order functions, such as learning, grow out of social interaction. It holds that our learning processes are products of our society and our culture. Different cultures have different systems, such as beliefs, values, behaviours, and practices which provide a context for learning. Therefore, to fully understand someone we must examine the external social world in which that person has developed.

Vygotsky was highly influential in sociocultural theory. He described learning as being embedded within social events and that learning takes place as a child interacts with the people, objects and events in that environment. Learning is therefore socially and culturally defined.

Documenting children's learning is another way of creating a narrative about what a child has done and achieved. Providing documentary evidence of children's learning recorded through observations and examples of children's work, usually kept as a portfolio or folder of which children and staff and parents can all contribute to, is well established in early years. Assessments of children's learning can be completed through careful analysis and interpretation of the documented evidence.

However, the approach in the Reggio Emilia schools has been highly influential in developing this practice. The way in which the Reggio Emilia schools document their children's learning focuses intensively on children's experience, memories, thoughts and ideas as they work. Documentation in Reggio Emilia typically include samples of a child's work at several different stages of completion; photographs showing work in progress; comments written by the practitioners working with the children; transcriptions of children's discussions, comments and explanations about the activity; and comments made by parents. Observations, transcriptions of tape-recordings, and photographs of children discussing are also included. Examples of the children's work and written reflections on the processes in which the children engaged are displayed in classrooms and corridors. This documentation reveals how the children planned, carried out and completed the displayed work (Katz and Chard, 1996).

It is important that in using different observational techniques to record and assess young children's learning practitioners are clear about the purpose of what they are doing and that the observational and recording processes are matched to this aim. Also, that the process enables practitioners to have a good understanding of what children know and can do, and through analysis and interpretation of observation and/or documentation they are able to adapt and refine their provision and pedagogical processes to best meet the needs of the children.

Read through the different observational techniques outlined.

- *Which observation technique, or combination of techniques, do you think would be best to learn about the aspects of children's learning and development listed below?*

- *What about timing? Which of these aspects of children's learning and development do you think will need to be assessed over a period of time to ensure a valid assessment of their abilities and needs is made?*

  - *A child's friendship group.*
  - *Which schemas a child is developing.*
  - *A child's creative development.*
  - *A child's well-being.*
  - *The development of a child's language for thinking.*
  - *A child's interests and preferences.*
  - *A child's physical development.*

- *Give reasons for your decisions.*

- *Are there any other ways of observing and recording children' learning that you are aware of that would be better suited to finding out about these aspects of children's learning and development?*

Observation-based assessment in the EYFS

Think about how your learning was assessed in senior school. For most subjects it would be through writing; perhaps essays or assignments or producing portfolios or written exams. This recording of what you know enabled your teachers to assess your learning. Young children do not yet have the skills to record their learning in this way. Young children's learning is evident through what they do, what they say, and when they record their learning it is likely to be in idiosyncratic ways. Therefore, we need to match how we find out about what children know and can do to the ways in which they represent their knowledge, skills and aptitudes. Observation-based assessment provides this opportunity. In observation-based assessment practitioners observe children and then, based on what they have observed, make an assessment of the child's learning and development. Observation allows practitioners to watch and make sense of children's learning in a naturalistic and fluid way. When being observed children are able to demonstrate how they make sense and meaning in their world through exploration and interaction in a situation that is familiar, developmentally appropriate and predominantly child-initiated. This enables the assessment of learning to be sensitively constructed around individual children. At best, this model of assessment is child-centred and focused on what happens next to support the child's learning and development.

ACTIVITY 3

- *Think back to the way that your learning was assessed in senior schools. How did teachers assess what you knew and could do?*

- *What are your views on this way of assessing learning?*

- *Describe what is meant by observation-based assessment.*

- *Why is this the way that young children's learning is assessed?*

- *Compare the two approaches.*

- *Who do you think benefits most within each approach? Give reasons for your response.*

When observation and assessment of children's play is done effectively it is done with compassion, recognising that the aim of observing children's learning is to see a child as an individual with strengths and needs. All children will come into settings with different experiences. These experiences will have had a direct impact on their learning and development. For some children their experiences will have supported their learning and development and they will have knowledge skills and aptitudes that are within expected developmental parameters. Other children's experiences will mean that they need time and opportunity to develop and learn within the setting before their development sits within expected developmental parameters. The purpose of observation-based assessment is to establish what children know and can do, and, to identify their needs so that provision and interaction can be matched to these needs. This makes observation-based assessment useful and appropriate. Assessment of children for the sole purpose of levelling and labelling is neither appropriate nor useful in early years settings. Ascribing levels and labels does only that: ascribe levels and labels; it is a poor indicator of what to do next to support children's learning and development. This is important. Assessment in early years settings needs to be predominantly formative, not summative.

Definitions	
Formative assessment	Assessment focused on producing information that is used to adapt provision to meet a child's needs. This is often referred to as *assessment **for** leaning*.
Summative assessment	Assessment focused on summarizing a child's learning and development at a particular point in time. This is often referred to as *assessment **of** learning*.

It is also important to be aware that, as practitioners, we make choices about what we observe and what we assess and realise that these choices indicate what we value in children and children's play. It is almost always practitioners who select what to observe, when to observe and where to observe children's learning, and we bring to that situation many assumptions about what is worthwhile observing. It is important therefore that we are aware of what assumptions and prejudices we hold about what constitutes worthwhile play and worthwhile activities and how this impacts on what, and how, and when we observe children. Where necessary we need to challenge these assumptions within ourselves and others to ensure that our observations of children reflect all of who they are.

We may also find ourselves only observing the easily observable, i.e. what children say and do. This is clearly an important part of observation but other aspects of who children are are equally important: their feelings, thoughts, attitudes and dispositions. How do we observe this? How do we ensure that our assessment of who children are and what they can do is holistic? To achieve this observation and assessment needs to be multi-dimensional, in both content and perspective. In this way we ensure that our assessments of children have breadth as well as depth and reflect the complexity of young children's learning and development. For example, practitioners may use the Mosaic approach (Clark and Moss, 2001) alongside a more traditional pattern of observation in order to include the child's perspective on themselves, their world, and their learning. These combined approaches enable us to have a more holistic understanding of who children are and what they can do.

The Mosaic approach to observing children's learning

The Mosaic approach (Clark and Moss, 2001) is a multi-method approach to bringing together children's own views of their lives and their pre-school setting. It aims for children to be participatory in constructing an understanding of their lives.

The approach uses a range of ways of 'listening' to children to construct this understanding of their lives:

- Observation. Children are listened to through observation based upon two questions: *what is it like to be here?* and *do you listen to me?*
- Discussion (child conferencing) with the child. This is based on a framework of 14 questions around the key themes of why children came to Nursery; the role of adults; favourite and worst activities and people.
- Use of cameras. Children take photographs of things that are important to them in the setting.
- Use of tours. A tour of the setting led by the child, again highlighting the things that are important to the child.
- Use of mapping. In discussion with the staff children use their photographs and aspects of the tour to record their views of the setting.

Assessment requirements in the EYFS

The Early Years Foundation Stage (DFE, 2012) requires that assessment of children's abilities and needs is achieved predominantly through observation-based assessment. It states that:

> ongoing assessment is an integral part of the learning and development process. It involves practitioners observing children to understand their level of achievement, interests and learning styles, and then to shape learning experiences for each child reflecting those observations.

(DFE, 2012, p.10).

It is expected that practitioners establish systems to ensure that children are observed regularly and assessments made of this learning are clearly used to support planning and provision. This process is known as formative assessment or assessment for learning.

ACTIVITY 4

Some challenges and dilemmas have been identified in developing an effective system for observation-based assessment.

- *Planning time for practitioners to complete regular observations of children. This is particularly difficult in settings when children attend on an irregular basis.*

- *Involving parents in contributing to the observation and assessment.*

- *Creating records that are clear and accessible to everyone who needs to see them.*

How could settings overcome these challenges?

1 *What have you seen in settings and schools that works?*

2 *What other ideas do you have?*

Summative assessment, or assessment of learning, is also required within the EYFS. There are two points in the Foundation Stage when there is a requirement that all settings, including those in the private voluntary and independent sectors who have received funding for pre-school education from the government, complete these summative assessments. Firstly, a progress check at two years old and secondly completion of the Foundation Stage Profile in the final term of the year in which the child reaches five years of age.

The first assessment, the progress check, is completed between the ages of 24 and 36 months. Practitioners must review children's progress in the prime areas and provide parents with a short written summary of their child's development. The progress check must identify the child's strengths, and any areas where the child's progress is less than expected. If there are significant emerging concerns, or an identified special educational needs or disability, practitioners need to plan to support future learning and development, alongside other professionals if needed.

Secondly, the Foundation Stage Profile must be completed for all children who are in their school/setting at the end of the Foundation Stage. For the vast majority of children the summative assessment will be completed in school at the end of their Reception year; the point at which they move into year one and the National Curriculum replaces the Early Years Foundation Stage. The profile should be completed from ongoing observations, all relevant records held by the setting, discussions with parents and any other adults who the teacher or parent judges can offer a useful contribution. The results of the assessment must be shared with parents and a copy of the profile given to the year one teacher together with a short commentary on each child's skills and abilities in relation to the three key characteristics of effective learning outlined in the EYFS (see Chapter 5 for more information on the assessment processes in the EYFS). This data must also be sent to the relevant local government authority. This information provides a data set used by schools, local authorities and government to track children's learning and development through their time in the education system.

A very small number of children may not do a Reception Year in school and remain in their nursery or playgroup until the end of the Foundation Stage. Where this happens the pre-school setting are responsible for completing the profile and meeting the requirements for sharing the information with the relevant people and authorities.

Settings may also be required to complete summative assessments of children's learning to inform processes of assessment where there is concern about a child or family. This is usually as part of broader assessment of the child's needs involving other agencies. This could be necessary at any point in a child's time in a setting or school.

CHAPTER SUMMARY

In this chapter we have explored why and how we observe and assess young children's learning. The importance of finding ways to observe, assess and record what children know and can do as starting points to adapt and modify provision and pedagogical practice is emphasised. Different techniques for observing, assessing and recording children's learning have been described and the importance of matching techniques to purpose highlighted. The observation and assessment requirements of the Early Years Foundation Stage are outlined.

FURTHER READING

Athey, C (1990) *Extending thought in young children.* London: Paul Chapman Publishing.

Athey, C (2007) *Extending thought in young children, 2nd edn.* London: Sage.

Carr, M (2001) *Assessment in early childhood settings: learning stories.* London: Sage.

Clark, A and Moss, P (2001) *Listening to young children.* London: National Children's Bureau.

DFE (2012) *Statutory Framework for the Early Years Foundation Stage.* DFE. **https://www.education.gov.uk/publications/standard/publicationDetail/Page1/DFE-00023-2012**

Drummond, MJ (1993) *Assessing children's learning.* London: David Fulton.

Featherstone, S, Bestwick, C and Louis S (2008) *Again! Again! Understanding schemas in young children.* London: Featherstone Education Ltd.

Glazzard, J, Chadwick, D, Webster, A and Percival, J (2010) *Assessment for learning in the Early Years Foundation Stage.* London: Sage.

Hobart, C and Frankel, J (1999) *A practical guide to observation and assessment.* Cheltenham: Nelson Thornes.

Hutchin, V (2007) *Supporting every child's learning across the Foundation Stage.* London: Hodder & Stoughton.

Katz, L and Chard, S (1996) *The contribution of documentation to the quality of early childhood education.* **www.cariboo.bc.ca/ae/literacies/reggio/reggioarticle1.htm**

Nutbrown, C (1999) *Threads of thinking. Young children learning and the role of early education.* London: Paul Chapman.

Smidt, S (2005) *Observing, assessing and planning for children in the early years.* London: Routledge.

Thornton, L and Brunton, P (2005) *Understanding the Reggio approach.* London: David Fulton.

Thornton, L, Brunton, P and Green, S (2007) *Bringing the Reggio approach to your early years practice.* London: David Fulton.

Section 4

Enhancing practice and understanding

9 Reflecting on children's learning and development

This chapter will enable you to understand:

- what is reflection;
- what is reflective learning;
- what is reflective practice;
- what is a reflective practitioner;
- different models of reflective practice;
- how reflection supports an understanding of children's learning and development;
- the importance of reflective learning for emancipatory professional development.

Introduction

This chapter is concerned with reflection. Reflection is a way of learning. It is a process of actively considering what we do, and why and how we do it, in order to better understand children's learning, and to further develop our professional knowledge and skill. Being reflective is an essential professional skill. It requires practitioners to engage in developing a deeper understanding of their work. This is important, for not only do practitioners need to be skilled at what they do but this needs to be based on a good understanding of children and their learning. This understanding will not only support their practice but it will enable practitioners to consider, to question, and, at times, to challenge demands that are made of them. This can be done from a position of strength when practitioner's knowledge and understanding of young children's learning has been carefully considered so practice is soundly based in active, considered and well-informed choices.

Reflection, reflective learning and reflective practice

What is reflection?

Reflection is a process of becoming aware of what you are doing and why you are doing it. It is a process of learning from your experiences. It is about being critically aware of yourself, your thoughts, action, language and interactions. It is about carefully and knowledgably analysing these processes and drawing evaluative conclusions about the what, how and why of your practice.

Reflection is an in depth consideration of events or situations by oneself or with critical support. The reflector aims to work out what has happened, what they thought or felt about it, why, who was involved and when. It is looking at whole scenarios from as many angles as possible: people, relationships, situation, place, timing, chronology, causality, and so on, to make situations and people more comprehensible. This involves reviewing or reliving the experience to bring it into focus.

(Bolton, 2005, p.9)

The process of reflection involves metacognition. Metacognition is the ability to be aware of and to think about and consider our own thinking. Metacognitive thinking often follows cognitive activity. Cognitive activity occurs as we observe and notice what is happening within an activity or experience and metacognitive activity occurs as we reflect on our thoughts, feelings and responses within what we noticed. Metacognition is a higher-order thinking process that has shown to be associated with successful learning (see Livingston, 1997).

What is reflective learning?

Reflective learning is the process of learning from reflecting. It is a process of learning through internally examining and exploring an issue triggered by an experience. This exploration leads to a clarification in meaning followed by a change in understanding (Boud, Keogh and Walker, 1985).

This purpose of reflective learning is to clarify your understanding of an activity or experience and your role in it. This professional knowledge can then inform your practice.

As well as this pragmatic approach to practice reflective learning can involve consideration of wider ethical and political choices within early years. Moss (2008) reminds us that all that we do in early years is underpinned by choice. For example, we can choose what image of the child we engage with, and we can aim to construct our own understanding of early years practice through questioning and interrupting the dominant discourse. Reflection and reflective learning can underpin a questioning approach to our work. By developing active, lively, questioning minds we give ourselves permission to develop our own understanding of early years, and, in doing this go beyond being technicians and become well-informed, thoughtful and self-defined practitioners.

Definition	
Dominant discourse	The expected ways of thinking, talking and understanding that we take for granted, and, that shape our ways of living and working. These ways of being are almost always determined by dominant, decision-making groups in a society.

What is reflective practice?

Reflective practice is the practice that flows from reflective learning. It is practice that is informed by a richer understanding of what you do because of your analysis of the context of early learning and of your own practice. In reflective practice changes flows from conscious though and learning. Changes in practice are made through purposeful noticing, thinking, analysing and evaluating.

Being a reflective practitioner

Reflection, reflective learning and reflective practice are all stages in the process of being a reflective practitioner. The requirement to be a reflective practitioner is threaded through current Early Years discourse (see Figure 9.1). Reed and Canning (2010, p.8) observe that *reflective practice is seen as having the potential to make a difference for children and families, as being significant for the way in which we respond to needs*. They point out that the ability to apply knowledge to experience in order to reflect upon and improve practice is embedded in a range of early years practice documentation.

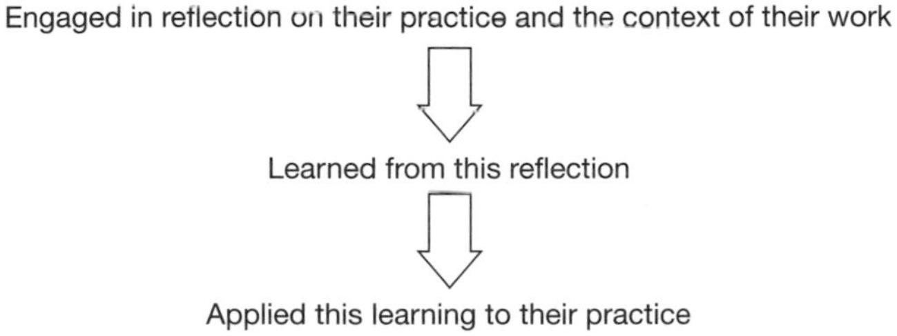

Engaged in reflection on their practice and the context of their work

⇩

Learned from this reflection

⇩

Applied this learning to their practice

Figure 9.1 A reflective practitioner

THEORY FOCUS

An adaptation of the Johari window

A useful way of understanding the process of bringing action in conscious awareness to reflect upon it is an adaptation of the Johari window, sometimes called a conscious competence matrix (Figure 9.2). In this model reflective learning would be a process of becoming conscious-competent at what you do to inform changes in practice.

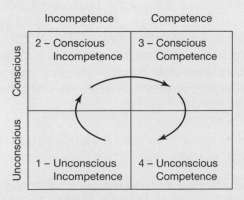

Figure 9.2 Conscious competence learning matrix

continued

Applying this model to an aspect of practice.

1 **Unconscious incompetence** – at this stage practitioners are unaware of the need for changes in an aspect of their practice.

2 **Conscious incompetence** – at this stage practitioners become aware of the need for changes in their practice.

3 **Conscious competence** – at this stage people are aware of what they are doing and aim to change and improve their practice through conscious noticing and reflecting upon what they do.

4 **Unconscious competence** – at this stage practitioners have reflected on their practice, developed their understanding and made changes to what they do. These changes then become embedded in their practice so practitioners no longer need to consciously focus on this aspect of their practice.

CASE STUDY

Georgia had just started a new job in a foundation unit in a school. Part of her role was to have a group of children for story time. This was something that she had done in her previous job. However, over the first few weeks Georgia began to realise that the children in her group became quickly restless during story time and that the strategies that she was using weren't successful in calming the group down. Georgia became increasingly aware that she needed to develop other strategies to engage the children at story time so that the session was a useful learning experience. She discussed this with the teacher. Together they decided that they would do three things: Georgia would observe the other staff's story times to see which strategies they were using; she would look for training opportunities that offered an understanding of and strategies for managing behaviour positively and effectively; she would read up about how young children learn and about effective practice in reading to young children. Once Georgia had considered what she had seen and read, and had a better understanding of the issue, they agreed that she would try some different strategies that she felt would work. The teacher would observe and support her in implementing them effectively. For a while Georgia had to think carefully about each session and actively plan which strategies she was going to use. However, as time passed the group became easier to engage and story times became calmer. Georgia could now respond effectively in the moment to any issues that arose.

Identify each of the four stages of learning in this case study.

- *How did Georgia become aware of her need to change her practice?*

- *What strategies did Georgia use to reflect on her practice?*

- *How did Georgia ensure that her reflective learning informed her practice?*

- *How did Georgia know that she had moved towards embedding her learning in her practice?*

ACTIVITY 1

Models of practice are best understood when applied to experiences, so think of an event or experience in your own life to explore this model.

1 How did you become aware of your need to learn more about an aspect of your life to enable you to become more competent?

2 What processes did you use to become more competent?

3 How much of this was a conscious cognitive process?

4 How did this process affect your ongoing competence in this area of your life?

Models of reflective practice

Engaging in reflective practice, and becoming a reflective practitioner, can be supported by models that explain and describe the process of reflection. Reflection is often divided into two distinct types – reflection-in-action and reflection-on-action (Schon, 1983). The distinction can be seen as one of timing and expertise.

Reflection-in-action

Reflection-in-action is the process of reflecting on practice during practice, and changing and adapting action and interaction in the moment according to need. This often happens at a subconscious level. At a basic level it is the rapid practical decision making that we do as we practice, for example: how to present activities and resources; which book to choose to read to a particular group of children; what to do when there is a dispute between children. For skilled and experienced practitioners these rapid decisions can be at a very sophisticated level. For example: during an activity moving between different interactive strategies to ensure that children remain engaged; knowing exactly when to change, alter or adapt provision to ensure children continue to be engaged and learn; responding to parents each day and adapting the tone of these interactions in the moment to meet their needs; judging whether to encourage a child to persist with an activity or not. These are quite complex judgements to make in the moment and require an excellent understanding of children, their learning and development and of pedagogical practice.

Reflection-on-action

Reflection-on-action involves consciously thinking about and considering practice after it has happened. This is done to understand what happened and to analyse and interpret what this means so that we can change future practice. Reflection-on-action is done retrospectively and allows time and space to engage with the processes of theory and practice. This implies that there are cognitive processes involved; cognitive processes of professional meaning-making that have an impact on how we perceive our role and what we do.

The process of reflection

The process of reflection on professional practice can be understood as a staged process. Jasper (2003) describes a five-stage approach.

1 Select an experience or activity to reflect upon.

2 Observe and describe what happens.

3 Analyse what happened.

4 Interpret what happened.

5 Explore alternatives.

6 Frame future action.

Select an experience

In practice the starting point for reflection is an event, experience or activity. There are a number of ways of selecting the area of practice for reflection.

• It could be in an area of your practice that you know that you want to understand better. You would then choose when to engage in this area of practice with the intention of observing reflecting and analysing your practice.

• It might occur to you during practice that this activity/event/experience is something that you want to explore further. This might be because it has gone very well and you want to understand why this was. It may occur to you as you are engaged in practice that this is an aspect of your practice that you need to develop.

• The starting point may be a critical incident. Brookfield (1990) describes critical incidents as situations or events that are vividly remembered and hold special significance for the person taking part. These incidents can be both positive and negative. What is important is that they feel significant for the individual – a moment in time from which to learn. The word critical, in this instance, means important or significant, a decisive moment or turning point. Critical incidents are also sometimes referred to as critical moments. Critical incidents/moments can act as excellent stimuli for reflection and learning.

ACTIVITY 2

Seeing the pattern – exploring how critical incidents or moments influence thoughts and action.

I can still recall the conversation with a friend, Rebecca, at school who said that she was going to be an infant school teacher. As she said it, it occurred to me, in that moment, that that was what I wanted to do. That for me was a critical moment on my career path.

• *Draw a simple timeline about how you came to be a reading about/studying early childhood development. What were the significant critical moments (conversations, events, experiences) that were important in your choice?*

• *Analyse how these moments influenced your choice. Keep focused on the analysis. In what ways did these critical moments influence your decision to read about/study child*

ACTIVITY *continued*

development? What decisions did you take following these critical moments? How did they influence what you did next?

- *What action flowed from those critical moments? What did you do that was different from before?*

Observe and describe what happens

The purpose of this stage of the process is to record, in as much detail as is necessary, what happened. This recording of what happened will be the material that you work from, and return to, in your reflection. Jasper (2003) recommends asking six questions of the event/experience as a framework for recording the detail of what happened; who, what, when, where, why, how.

This recording can be done in many ways, including:

- a formal observation;
- an informal observation;
- as a conversation;
- tape-recorded;
- photographs;
- as a video recording;
- as a journal – written or pictorial or an electronic journal such as a blog;
- as a graphic (pictorial representation).

You will need to make sure that the way in which you record your work complies with the rules and permissions that govern working with children.

The important aspect of recording is that it provides sufficient content and stimulus to enable you analyse what happened accurately and in depth. How you record will depend upon the context in which you are undertaking reflection, and, your preferred way of conceptualising and recording what you have seen and experienced. For some people this will be through the written word; others will prefer to represent things visually and use pictorial representation. Some people are more comfortable with electronic recording and representation. It is, of course, possible to use a range of methods to record what has happened. What is important is that this is shaped into something that has meaning for you and offers a stimulus to thought.

Analyse what happened

At this stage in the reflective process you start to explore what happened in order to understand what happened. This is what analyse means: to study something in detail in order to discover more about it. The process of analysis requires that you think deeply and systematically about what happened. It also requires that you make links between what you know about Early Years practice and the situation that you are analysing. This may involve you in finding out more to inform your analysis, as you need to have sufficient knowledge and understanding to support your analysis.

Interpret what happened

What should emerge in this stage of the reflective process is a clear understanding of the event, experience or activity – an interpretation based on your analysis. Your aim is now to construct an understanding that has meaning for you and your professional practice. Your interpretation of what happened needs to be cohesive as this will be a starting point for exploring what to do next. This can be achieved alone through thinking and reflecting on what you have learned, or it may be useful at this stage to work alongside someone else to discuss and interpret your understanding of what happened and apply this to your professional role.

Explore alternatives

You now have an understanding and interpretation of a particular aspect of your practice. The next stage in the reflective process is to open this knowledge up and explore the possibilities that it offers. Jasper (2003) talks about this process in terms of refocusing in order to see things in a different way, consciously seeking to see the features of our experience differently in order to learn and make changes. This exploration offers a range of possibilities for changes to perspective or practice, or building upon and developing successful practice, and acts as precursor to deciding exactly what change to make.

Frame future action

This stage of the reflective process involves a conscious process of seeking to apply what you have learned in the reflective process, both in terms of how you think and what you do. You may find that you have articulated a number of possibilities for change and you will need to consider these in terms of what is possible. These don't have to be big changes; small changes are often as effective as dramatic ones. Once you have made your choice about the way forward you need to commit to this particular change and consider how it can be integrated into your practice.

THEORY FOCUS

Changing practice

A useful model for understanding the process of and embedding change in your practice is the AFGAM model – a model from learning theory. Acquiring new skills and embedding them in practice takes time. It is not a case of either having skill or not having skill. This model offers a way of understanding the developmental progression of change.

Accuracy – this is the process of learning and developing accuracy in what you want to achieve.
Fluency – practising and becoming fluent in the skill.
Generalisation – able to use the skill fluently in different contexts.
Automatisation – the skill becomes automatic – learning the skill is over and it is embedded in practice.
Maintainance – maintaining the skill by doing it regularly.

ACTIVITY 3

Look at the AFGAM model in the Theory Focus box.

- Consider learning to drive. How does learning to drive fit into the model?

- Consider learning to skate. How does learning to skate fit into the model?

- Consider learning to read a story to a group of children. Map this to the model.

- Consider another skill that you have acquired. Map your learning to the model. Which stage was the most challenging? Why do you think this is?

The reflective process is most effective when it is an ongoing process. This means that once you have framed your action and changed your practice this change then becomes the subject for further reflection. In this way we continue to learn and deepen our understanding of our professional practice and develop our understanding of Early Years.

Reflecting on issues

The process of reflecting upon an issue, rather than an aspect of practice, will be similar in terms of the processes of analysis, interpretation and exploration of alternatives. However, when dealing with an issue rather than an aspect of practice, the second stage, of observation and description, is likely to be replaced by reading and discussion to enable you to be well informed before undertaking analysis and interpretation of the issue. Similarly, stage six, framing the future, is likely to be in terms of perspective, understanding and approach rather than a concrete example of changed practice. This is also an ongoing process of developing a questioning and well informed response to the context of our professional practice.

ACTIVITY 4

At what age should children start statutory school?

This is an issue that invokes lively debate in early years. The starting age of five years was established in the 1876 Elementary Education Act. It is not made clear in the act why the age of five was chosen. The age for leaving school has been altered and changed many times, but not the starting age. Many other European countries have later starting ages and there is no evidence to suggest that this has negative impact on their educational attainment. Should we reconsider statutory school age?

- *Use the reflective learning process to consider this issue.*

You will need to analyse and interpret the available evidence and be aware of possible alternatives before drawing conclusions about what you consider to be an appropriate age at which children should start statutory school.

Clearly this reflective approach can be used in many different ways and in different situations: in our professional and personal lives; individually or within groups and teams of people; in relation to personal practice, practice across a team, or wider political policy and practice issues. In all situations the process and the aim will be the same; to notice, analyse and interpret something that has happened, or an issue that has arisen, and then explore alternative ways of responding to this which leads to changes in perspective and/or behaviour.

How does reflection support our understanding of children's learning and development?

The knowledge and skill of practitioners has been shown to be linked to the outcomes of children. The Effective Provision of Pre-school Education (EPPE) study (Sylva et al., 2003) and the Researching Effective Pedagogy in the Early Years (REPEY) study (Siraj-Blatchford et al., 2002) are clear that the quality of staffing in a setting (measured by level of qualification) is associated with the quality of provision and better cognitive outcomes for children. The importance of this in the reflective process is that as reflective learning has an impact on the knowledge and skill of staff it will, in turn, have an impact on the quality of provision. The quality of provision is likely to be enhanced as effective reflective learning makes explicit links between ideas, theories and expertise, provision and pedagogical approaches which, in turn, means that practitioners have a better understanding of provision and pedagogy and, importantly, how this is manifested in provision. This will enhance the quality of provision in a setting.

The reflective process can also be used directly to better understand individual children's learning. A practitioner may choose to focus the reflective process on a particular child's learning and development within an area of learning, or, focus on better understanding how a child learns best. The resulting analysis, interpretation and action are likely to lead to provision and pedagogical strategies that are closely aligned to the child's needs.

CASE STUDY

Reflecting on learning and applying learning theory

As key person to Sam, Jean decided to complete a time sample of observations with the intention of finding out which activities and experiences Sam was choosing during a session. She undertook a number of observations over a period of two weeks recording where Sam was playing, who he was playing with and how he engaged in play. Jean used the reflective process to consider Sam's learning.

Jean's analysis of the observations showed a number of things.

- *Sam played with a range of activities.*
- *He often played alongside Alex.*

- *Sam chose to play outside for part of each session.*

- *Sam seemed to enjoy small-world play and would become engrossed in his play, appearing to be acting out narratives with the toys.*

- *Sam's learning and development were appropriate for his age and experience.*

- *Sam played predominantly alone for most of each session. He rarely interacted with the other children and seemed content to do so.*

Jean's interpretation of the evidence was that Sam was settled and happy at Nursery. He appeared to be learning and developing well and had made progress since starting at Nursery school. Sam was content with his own company and his level of engagement in play was high. Jean had some concern that the observation evidence showed that Sam was spending a lot of time playing alone and wondered whether this was the best way for him to learn. She recalled Vygotsky's work on the importance of social interaction and peer support in learning and considered whether Sam might be missing out on one important way of learning. She also considered the work of Piaget and noted that Sam became deeply engaged in his play and it was evident that he was thinking and working things out in the scenarios that he created. Also that he accessed a range of activities that offered him opportunities to be explore and engage with learning in a dynamic and multi-sensory way.

In discussion with her colleagues Jean explored several possibilities of how to respond to what she had observed. One option was to not to intervene at this point; to leave Sam playing predominantly alone as he appeared content and was learning, but to be aware that this was something that she needed to keep in mind in later observation and reflection. Another possibility was to alter the provision to provide more opportunities for Sam, and the other children, to select more interactive activities. This may encourage Sam to choose activities that supported his learning through interaction. Thirdly she considered whether joining in Sam's play and encouraging him to interact during his play both with herself and other children. Lastly, she considered planning adult-led activities that she would engage Sam and Alex in, as he was the child Sam appeared to be most often playing alongside.

Jean decided to do two things: firstly, to alter provision to provide more opportunities for Sam and the other children to engage in interactive play, and to monitor Sam's response to this, and, secondly, to do some observations on Sam's language and social development, and speak with his parents, to make sure that there were no concerns about his development that may affect his social interaction. She decided on this course of action because, on reflection, she was aware that children learn in different ways and her observations showed that Sam appeared to be highly engaged in his play and was learning and developing well. Sam was happy and settled in the Nursery and appeared enjoy his time there. She surmised that perhaps this was Sam's preferred way to learn.

Reflective learning and emancipatory professional development

Reflective learning is a useful and effective way to enhance professional practice. However, there is an inherent danger in reflective learning; that it becomes a tool for us to turn ourselves into excellent technicians, able to deliver prescribed practices and procedures in the most effective way. Moss (2008) highlights this danger and offers us a choice, of choosing to become technicians or to determine our own ways of understanding and being in our professional roles. The inherent danger is that unless we offer ourselves the permission to articulate our own understandings and define how we practice, the power of external forces, outlined in policy and guidance, and embedded in much professional development training, will determine this for us. Clearly, there is much to commend in policy, guidance, and training but our orientation towards it is vital. We can choose whether to accept all that is demanded of us and aim to deliver it well, or, we can choose to develop our own understanding of effective practice and use this as a starting point to develop our own practice and, at times therefore, to question and filter demands that are made of us. Emancipatory professional practice flows from the construction of our own practice relatively free from demands and restrictions. Practice, in this model, emerges from a strong and detailed understanding of how children learn and of effective pedagogical practice. Practice developed in this way can then be highly contextualised and therefore made relevant for each particular group of children.

The process of reflection is important in understanding and constructing effective early years practice. If we offer ourselves permission to use reflection to consider our practice then we have an effective tool to develop and construct our professional practice within a community of early years practitioners.

C H A P T E R   S U M M A R Y

In this chapter we have considered reflection as an important way of developing professional practice and of understanding how children develop and learn. We have explored what is meant by reflection, reflective learning and reflective practice, and the importance of becoming a reflective practitioner. A staged model of the reflective process has been detailed. The inherent danger of using reflection to become effective early years technicians rather than early years practitioners has been discussed.

FURTHER READING

Ball, S (2008) *The education debate. Policy and politics in the twenty first century.* Bristol: Policy Press.

Bolton, G (2005) *Reflective practice. Writing and professional development.* 2nd edition. London: Sage.

Boud, D, Keogh, R and Walker, D (1985) *Reflection: turning learning into experience.* London: Paul Chapman.

Brookfield, S (1990) Using critical incidents to explore leavers' assumptions, in J Mezirow and associates (eds) *Fostering critical reflection in adulthood.* San Francisco: Josey-Bass.

DFES (2005) (KEEP) *Key elements of effective practice.* **www.teachernet.gov.uk/docbank/index.cfm?id=11033**

Ecclestone, K and Hayes, D (2009) *The dangerous rise of therapeutic education.* London: Routledge.

Furedi, F (2003) *Therapy culture. Creating vulnerability in an uncertain age.* London: Routledge.

Guldberg, H (2009) *Reclaiming childhood. Freedom and play in an age of fear.* London: Routledge.

Jasper, M (2003) *Beginning reflective practice.* Cheltenham: Nelson Thornes.

Livingston, J (1997) *Metacognition. An overview.* **http://gse.buffalo.edu/fas/shuell/CEP564/Metacog.htm**

Louv, R (2005) *Last child in the woods. Saving our children from nature-deficit disorder.* Chapel Hill North Carolina. Algonquin Books.

Moss, P (2008) in Paige-Smith A and Craft A (2008) *Developing reflective practice in the early years.* Berkshire: Open University Press.

Moss, P and Petrie, P (2002) *From children's services to children's spaces. Public policy, children and childhood.* London: Routledge Falmer.

Moyles, J (2010) *The excellence of play.* Buckinghamshire: Open University Press.

Paige-Smith, A and Craft, A (2008) *Developing reflective practice in the early years.* Berkshire: Open University Press.

Palmer, S (2007) *Toxic childhood.* London: Orion.

Reed, M and Canning, N (2010) *Reflective practice in the early years.* London: Sage.

Schon, D (1983) *The reflective practitioner. How professionals think in action.* London: Temple Smith.

Siraj-Blatchford I, Sylva, K, Muttock, S, Gilden, R and Bell, D (2002) *Researching Effective Pedagogy in the Early Years.* (REPEY) *Research Report.* DFES RR356. **www.dfes.gov.uk/research/data/uploadfiles/RR356.pdf**

Sylva, K, Melhuish, E, Sammons, P, Siraj-Blatchford, I, Taggart, B and Elliot, K (2003) *Effective Provision of Pre-School (EPPE) Project: Findings from the Pre-School Period.* **http://eppe.ioe.ac.uk/eppe/eppefindings.htm**

10 Thinking, questioning and challenging: a critical approach to the early years

This chapter enables you to:

- understand what is meant by a critical approach to early years;
- consider examples of a critical approach to early years;
- explore a critical approach to developmentalism.

Introduction

In the previous chapter we considered what it means to be a reflective practitioner. The final section in that chapter discussed the possibilities of reflective learning as a way of shaping our own professional knowledge. This chapter extends that idea and discusses the importance of adopting a critical stance: asking questions, challenging assumptions and seeking understandings to support our professional practice.

What is meant by a critical approach to early years?

When we enter a profession there is a significant body of knowledge and skill that we need to acquire. This consists of how to do our job and the underpinning knowledge that is required to understand what we do. We learn this from others who work in the field. This package of knowledge and skill has been developed over a period of time in the context of philosophical, social and cultural understandings, and, additionally in education, the policies of various governments who seek to influence society through settings, schools and schooling.

But where does this knowledge, skill and guidance come from? Who decides what knowledge and which skills are important? Who are the 'experts' in this field? Is something the right thing to do just because it has been understood and done like this for a long time? Is something right because it in government documentation and guidance? What is the role of the practitioner? How do practitioners decide what is important to know, understand and do?

These questions are highly significant in understanding and shaping early years provision. If we, as practitioners, are to fully understand and be involved in shaping early years practice and provision we need to adopt a critical stance towards our professional role. 'Critical' in this context means to be analytical and evaluative, rather than to criticise. It means to stay alive to possibilities, to evaluate what we read or what we are told or asked or required to do. It means that we need to think, to question, to challenge, to adapt, to seek out understandings, and from that formulate a deep understanding of our professional role that flows from our own thoughts, commitments and knowledge rather than just accept the one that is given to us by others, and required from us in statutory frameworks.

Why is it important to develop a critical approach to professional knowledge, understanding and skill?

There are a number of reasons why it is important to engage in analysing and evaluating professional knowledge and skill.

- **Knowledge is created**. In the field of early childhood, knowledge is created. It alters, changes and develops over time as we learn more about how children learn and develop and how we can support their learning. A body of knowledge like this is often referred to as a discourse. So we have a discourse about children and early childhood that shapes the ways in which we understand and talk about children and childhood. This in turn affects how we practise. The knowledge within this discourse is created in a number of ways, for example: in the theories of child development that are prominent in the field; through the influence of pioneering figures; through research evidence in this field and others; through knowledge generated in practice; through social and cultural expectations and norms; and through political agendas. This knowledge finds its way into practice through the dissemination of knowledge in books, journals and magazines, in training courses and degree programmes, through professional development opportunities, and in government guidance and statutory requirements. As practitioners we have a choice: we can choose to accept all that we read, are told, asked and required to do or we can contribute to our understanding and skill through our own endeavours, through a desire to question and understand what we do and why. These can be questions about our day-to-day practice but are also likely to involve further questions in which we begin to analyse and evaluate wider understandings that create and maintain our professional role and identity.

- **Early years practitioner voices should be important in the discourse of early years**. This analytical and evaluative approach to our professional role is likely to be framed by the current discourse around children and childhood so it is worth considering who is generating this discursive framework. Where does the information that informs discussion and influences practice in early years come from? Who creates the knowledge? Who influences what practitioners in settings actually do? There is a tendency for all of us to imbue figures of authority with many qualities. This may of course be true, and the advice and expertise of others can be worth listening to, but there are also other voices in early years: practitioners. So what does it mean for an early years practitioner to put all of this 'expertise,' guidance and requirements into practice. What works? What doesn't? What could be even better? Adopting and analytical and evaluative approach to our work enables us to begin to answer these questions and to begin to develop our own understandings of what we do, understandings that mediate what we are taught and, in practice, what 'comes through the door.'

- **There are some fundamental questions that underpin early years which we need to have thought through**. A critical approach to our professional role will enable us to engage with important issues that underpin early years practice and provision. Many important issues are often decided beyond settings and practitioners react and respond to the decisions; for example, changes in the EYFS, research evidence about an aspect of practice, a professional development course that introduces a particular way of working. If we have thought through and formulated our own understandings about early years practice and provision we can use this understanding and commitment as a filter about what we are asked or required to do, or what we see, hear or read. For example, the revised EYFS (DFE, 2012) requires that there is a change in the balance of provision as a child reaches the end of Foundation Stage, towards more adult-led activities in preparation for school. If we are analytical rather than accepting of this change in the EYFS we realise that this raises fundamental questions about what early years education is for. What purpose does early years have? Are we just preparing children for school? Or, does the early years have some intrinsic value beyond the next stage? Should there be a balance between the two? If so, what balance? Who should decide this? How do these understandings impact on practice? Who decides this? Who is making these decisions? Why? What is the thinking behind it? You need to have thought things through and come to your professional role able to make professional judgements with considered knowledge, not just acquired knowledge.

ACTIVITY **1**

Think about your own early years knowledge.

- *Where did you acquire it?*

- *Who from?*

- *Why were they considered 'experts' in the field?*

- *How much do you rely on others and how much do you contribute to your own understanding?*

- *Which aspects of your knowledge and/or practice do you adopt a critical approach towards?*

Adopting a critical approach to early years practice

Throughout the activities in this book you have been asked to adopt a critical approach; to think through what the various ideas, requirements and guidance mean for you as a practitioner. You have been asked to take an evaluative stance, not to accept what you have been told but to think through what it really means for you, what you think and understand about what you have read in this text and what it means for you as a practitioner.

For example, in Chapter 5 you were asked to think about three different aspects of the Early Years Foundation Stage and asked to consider their implications for early years practice.

1 The EYFS development matters guidance states: *children develop at their own rates and in their own ways*.

2 There is an expectation that most children will achieve the Early Learning Goals by the time they reach the end of the Foundation Stage.

3 The developmental charts are written linked to broad ages and stages.

If we adopt an evaluative approach to these aspects of the EYFS we can see that it would be difficult to accept all of these statements together as there are tensions in what they say. How can it be that we know children develop at their own rates and in their own ways and yet there are a series of goals that most children are expected to reach by the chronological age of five? Also, what is the purpose of age/stage related development charts if we acknowledge that children develop at different rates and in their own ways? How as a practitioner do you work with this?

This example raises fundamental questions about developmentalism. What is it? Why do we use it? What for? What are the benefits? What challenges does it present? What do we need to know and consider as we work within a developmental approach, including the development matters guidance in the EYFS?

Understanding developmentalism

A developmental approach refers to the way of understanding of children's learning and development as a series of established patterns and sequences often linked to expectations of the age range at which children are likely to reach the stated level of learning. A developmental approach is widely used across all services for children. This approach clearly has benefits in informing the assessment of children abilities and needs to enable access to relevant services. However, there are also significant concerns about the uses of developmental assessment in childhood.

The benefits of a developmental approach

Categorising and describing development within different areas and in a hierarchical structure is a way of understanding and managing information about the expected pace, progress and sequence of children's learning and development. This enables people who work with children and their families to identify a child's abilities and needs and, when there are concerns about progress, focus on the identified need(s) and/or enable appropriate services or interventions to be identified and used to support the child's development. The case study below highlights how this can work in practice. It identifies the benefits of working in this way.

CASE STUDY

Using developmental expectations to assess and identify children's abilities and needs

Four-year-old Raoul had been at nursery for a couple of months. Staff always allowed this time for the children to settle before they did a series of formal observations to get to know, and record, the children's abilities and needs.

The staff had been making informal observations of Raoul since he had come to nursery and, informally, had observed that his pattern of language and communication was unusual.

They therefore decided to focus some observations on Raoul's language to create a clear profile of his abilities and needs. To support them in doing this they used the Early Years Foundation Stage development matters (2012) documents, that identify patterns and sequences of development linked to age ranges, and developmental progress charts from Sheridan (2008).

The staff undertook a series of observations over a week, observing Raoul in free play, at group times and during routines in the nursery. At the end of the week they met together and identified the patterns that they had observed in Raoul's language.

- *According to developmental expectations he had quite sophisticated language use for his age but seemed to have difficulties with finding words.*
- *He spoke very, very quietly.*
- *He sometimes spoke through his teeth without moving his mouth.*
- *Sometimes he withdrew completely and wouldn't speak.*
- *When an adult asked him to repeat what he had said as they hadn't heard him he wouldn't speak.*
- *In line with developmental expectations he used pronouns inconsistently, for example, used both 'me' and 'you' when referring to himself.*
- *He repeated phrases he had heard in order to request e.g. he would say 'Do you want a drink' to mean 'I want a drink.'*
- *He would understand things in a literal way, for example, when the children were tidying up a member of staff said 'Come on, jump to it' and he had responded 'I don't want to jump' and another time a member of staff had dropped some paint and said 'Whoops, look what I've done. I'll have to pull my socks up' and Raoul had commented 'but you're not wearing any socks.'*

The staff agreed that some of the ways in which Raoul used language was developmentally appropriate for his age. However, despite this, staff remained concerned that other aspects of his language didn't conform to expectations, and the frequency and persistence of the issues they had observed led them to agree that they needed to seek further advice.

Staff knew that they didn't have the necessary expertise to understand Raoul's needs well enough to put things in place in the nursery. They agreed that the teacher would speak with Raoul's dad when he came to pick him to ask about their experiences of Raoul's talking at home, and to ask for consent to seek further advice on how to support Raoul's language development at nursery.

Developmentalism and early intervention

A developmental approach is also used in early intervention. One of the current emphases in early years is early intervention. This is a process whereby children whose development falls outside of expected parameters or who are predicted as likely to need additional support to maintain developmental progress are offered the additional support. This may take the form of a place in a nursery, longer hours in a nursery, classes, workshops and programmes for parents, access to resources such as a toy library, or access to additional services from professional such a speech and language therapists. The aim of early intervention is to ensure that children's development is maintained in the years before they enter statutory schooling. Recent reports have identified benefits of early intervention for both the child, the family and wider society (Allan, 2011; Field, 2010).

Early intervention relies on a developmental approach in a number of ways.

- It is used in the assessment of a child's abilities and needs.

- Where a lack of development can be shown it provides a justification for additional money and resources.

- Developmental progress is one of the ways in which outcomes of the interventions are often justified and measured.

A developmental approach thus provides concrete, measurable ways of assessing children, justifying services and resources and measuring outcomes of early years work. This is an example of a straightforward way of using developmental psychology to support our understanding of children's needs and focus services where they are needed.

THEORY FOCUS

Early intervention

In 2011 Graham Allan MP led a review on early intervention. The review team's core message was that early intervention is a approach that offers our country a real opportunity to make lasting improvements in the lives of our children, to forestall many persistent social problems and end their transmission from one generation to the next and to make long-term savings in public spending (Allan, 2011, p.vii).

Early intervention is identified as general approaches and specific policies and programmes which help give children aged 0–3 the social and emotional bedrock they need to reach their full potential; and to approaches that help older children become the good parents of tomorrow. The rationale behind this is that many of the costly and damaging social problems in society and created because we are not giving children the right support in their earliest years, when they should achieve their most rapid development. Allan (2011) argues that if we do not provide that help early enough, then it is often too late. As justification for this claim he outlines evidence that supports the importance of a child's earliest years:

continued

- The first two years are crucial for a child's brain development. A key finding is that babies are born with 25 per cent of their brains developed, and there is then a rapid period of development so that by the age of three their brains are 80 per cent developed.

- A child's development score at 22 months can serve as an accurate predictor of educational outcomes at 26 years.

- An authoritative study of boys assessed by nurses at age three as being 'at risk' found that they had two and half times more criminal convictions by the age of 21 as compared to the group deemed as not being at risk. Additionally, in the 'at risk' group 55 per cent of the convictions were for violent offences, compared to 18 per cent in the not at risk group.

In addition to benefits to the child and family there are economic benefits for the country. Allan (2011) cites evidence from America that early intervention with children and families deemed to be at risk has cost benefits: reduced benefits and criminal justice expenditure, higher tax revenues and reduced health costs because of the improved physical and mental health of the people involved.

The report recognises that, whilst we can understand and map the benefits of early intervention, the more difficult task is to ensure and that all services work together in ways that best meet the needs of children and families, and that funding is available to facilitate this.

However, as well a developmental approach having observable benefits, if we adopt a critical stance there are other perspectives that need to be considered: ones that raise questions and challenge underpinning assumptions within this approach.

Critiques of a developmental approach

Definitions	
Critique	critical analysis
Critical analysis	an appraisal based on careful analytical evaluation

One way of understanding all theory, including child development theory, is to see it as a filter through which we form our view of the world. The theory acts like a filter so it allows some things to be perceived and others not. This allows only some aspects of the world to impact on our understanding as we seek to interpret and understand that which we perceive. Developmental patterns and sequences based on child development theory, whilst useful in some ways, act as such a filter. They provide a concrete, observable and easily understood framework to understand children and childhood. However, precisely because certain aspects of a child's development are concrete, observable and easier to understand, this, some argue, obscures other aspects of how children grow and learn, and therefore judgements are made about children based on what we can observe rather than what ideally we need to know.

Developmentalism is a view of human life in which new abilities are thought to unfold in sequential steps or be acquired in a series of stages (Baker, 1999). Dahlberg et al. (1999) agree; they describe the child within child development theory as the scientific child of biological stages. This child is one whose development, regardless of context, follows a standard trajectory of often age related stages. It is a child who is viewed as a series of identifiable and measurable areas of development: social, intellectual, physical, and linguistic. It is a child who is viewed as one of a kind: a universal being waiting to be realised (James and Prout, 1997). Development in this conceptualisation of children is understood as an internal process, supported by others, but essentially individual.

Age-related stages of development, such as the developmental matters in the EYFS, are informed by developmental psychology and are thus based on the same assumptions. Development is assumed to be linear, staged progression linked to chronological age. It doesn't, in this form, take any account of a child's individual learning experiences. The charts lists norms: developmental parameters which can be used to make assessments of children's progress and check whether they match age related descriptions. As aforementioned, this use of developmental ages and stages has clear practical use in the systems of health, education and social care as they are currently constructed, however, this form of assessment of children's abilities and needs also raises significant concerns.

ACTIVITY 2

Assessing developmental progress

Joe, Mazara and Sophie are all five years old and reaching the end of the Foundation Stage. In preparation for completing the Foundation Stage Profile, and their move into Year 1 in school, their communication and language development has been assessed and mapped to the development matters statements in the EYFS (DFE, 2012).

Joe's development is in accordance with his chronological age.

Mazara and Sophie are both able to use language to widen contacts, to share feelings, experiences and thoughts and can use a variety of questions. This is typical development for a child aged between 22 and 36 months.

- *Based on these outcomes, what is your assessment of these children's language development?*

- *State the reasons for your view.*

Now read these pen portraits of the children.

Joe is an only child of older parents. His mother has been at home with him. Before coming to school Joe and his mother have attended a range of groups; playgroups, singing groups and gym-tots. He arrived at school confident, able to talk with adults and children and keen to be involved in all the activities on offer.

Mazara came to England with her parents six months ago. Her parents are both surgeons at the local hospital. They both speak fluent English but they have decided to speak Urdu at home with Mazara so that she maintains her home language. When she arrived in England Mazara spoke no English.

continued

Sophie has specific learning difficulties which affect her understanding of language and her ability to speak fluently and clearly. She thoroughly enjoys nursery particularly role-play. She is good friends with Joe. A speech and language therapist supports Sophie and the staff in the Nursery.

- *What is your assessment of these children's language development having read the background information?*
- *What has made a difference to your assessment?*
- *What do these case studies add to your understanding of each child?*
- *Why is this context important in assessing children's developmental progress and attainment?*

The most persistent criticism of developmentalism is the one highlighted above: that it is decontextualised. That is, it doesn't allow for the different contexts in which children grow and learn. Developmentalism seeks to identify very broad, general patterns of development and apply these to all children regardless of their life experiences. Therefore, critics argue, that the approach is too unsubtle to understanding every child's growth and development. Additionally, there is the risk that normative descriptions of children's development provided by developmental psychology become prescriptions for what 'should' happen and judgements are made about children based on these assumptions. Burman (2008) and Baker (1999) identify the potential impact of this.

- Normative descriptions are used to classify and stratify individuals, groups and societies. When developmental parameters are articulated and set down the visibility of expectations means that children can be segregated into those who meet expectations and those who don't. Thus, by intention or default, we create inclusion and exclusion.

- Normative descriptions inform interventions to mould children into appropriate future citizens (Burman, 2008). There are clear links between this concern and the notion of 'early intervention'.

Burman (2008) argues that we need to think carefully very about these wider implications of a developmental approach, that we need unpick, or deconstruct, the understandings that lie behind the approach. She is not challenging the detail of the theories that underpin developmental ages and stages but asking that we become aware of the ways in which these are used in society, that is these wider meanings and uses of developmentalism in society that are problematic.

Burman's critical analysis questions the assumption of developmental psychology as 'the truth.' She argues that there are a range of ideological assumptions within developmentalism that reflect a wider socio-political agenda.

- Whose development is being described and used as the measure for all children? Is it all children in all contexts? All classes, all cultures, girls and boys? If not, whose development has prominence and whose is not considered in the ages and stages outlined as developmental norms?

Gilligan's work, outlined in the theory focus below, is a good example of this tension.

* Who is subject to intervention when developmental milestones are judged to have not been met?

Burman (2008) argues that it is the adequacy of mothering that developmental psychology is, in practice, used to judge. This is evidenced in the interventions that are designed to intervene and normalise children's development through services for children. In this way a developmental approach is used to regulate families, mothers in particular, because a 'good mother' is defined in relation to her child in the context of the child's developmental progress. This seems particularly pertinent if patterns of developmental progress used privilege some groups over others.

Burman (2008) reflects that *we need to be vigilant about the range of intended and unintended effects mobilised by claims to development, mindful of whose development is being privileged and correspondingly, whose is marginalised* (p. 12).

THEORY FOCUS

Moral development

An example of an unintended effect of developmental theory.

Kohlberg (1973), in developing his theory of moral development, presented 72 boys aged between ten and thirteen with a moral dilemma. He was interested in their reasoning behind their responses to the dilemma. From this reasoning he developed a stages theory of moral development which has been widely accepted. The stages are hierarchical.

Level 1 – Pre-conventional morality
      Stage 1 – obedience and punishment orientation
      Stage 2 – Individualism and exchange

Level 2 – Conventional morality
      Stage 3 – Good interpersonal relationships
      Stage 4 – Maintaining the social order

Level 3 – Post-conventional morality
      Stage 5 – Social contract and individual rights
      Stage 6 – Universal principles

Level 1 – At stage 1 children think of what is right is that which authority says is right. Doing the right thing is obeying authority and avoiding punishment. At stage 2, children see that there are different sides to any issue. Since everything is relative, one is free to pursue one's own interests, although it is often useful to make deals and exchange favours with others.

Level 2 – At stages 3 and 4, young people think as members of the conventional society with its values, norms, and expectations. At stage 3, they emphasise being a good person,

continued

THEORY FOCUS continued

which means having helpful motives toward people to whom you are close. At stage 4, the concern shifts toward obeying laws to maintain society as a whole.

Level 3 – At stages 5 and 6 people are less concerned with maintaining society for its own sake, and more concerned with the principles and values that make for a good society. At stage 5 they emphasise basic rights and the democratic processes that give everyone a say, and at stage 6 they define the principles by which agreement will be just.

This understanding of morality has been criticised by Gilligan (1982). Gilligan says that the stages are sex-biased. She observes that Kohlberg's stages were developed exclusively from interviews with males and therefore embed a male view of morality that centres around rules, rights and abstract principles.

Gilligan's work demonstrates that women's morality centres much more around interpersonal relationships and the ethics of care, compassion and maintaining relationships. It is about real, lived, ongoing relationships and the associated ways of living that achieve this rather than abstract ideas. Therefore, in Kohlberg's stages of moral development women score typically at stage three, whilst the highest stages are reserved for more male ways of thinking.

ACTIVITY 3

Make sure that you have read and understood the theory focus above.

- Why, in Gilligan's (1982) view, do Kohlberg's moral developmental levels mean that women are likely to achieve a lower level of development than men?

- What are the implications of this?

- How is context important in Gilligan's conclusions?

- What parallels can you see with Gilligan's work and the use of a developmental approach in early years?

- What are the implications of this?

Conclusion

The issues highlighted above are complex and not easily addressed. There is clearly a need within services for children to manage and provide for children's differing needs. A developmental approach provides a way of making differences visible and this supports the process of decision-making. But, as Baker (1999) notes, is developmentalism a sufficiently sophisticated approach to be left in singular charge of the multiple and diverse human population? If not, what are the alternatives? Even those who would desire a different approach acknowledge that a psychological approach to children's development is so deeply embedded in our ways of working with children that it is difficult to envisage alternatives. Indeed, some argue, it is almost impossible to posit alternatives without reference to psychology (Rose, 1996). So, foreseeably, developmentalism is likely to remain the dominant way in which we make judgements about children's progress, and information that we use to make judgements about services and the allocation of resources. Thus, practitioners in early years whose role often requires that they make normative developmental assessments, the pertinent issue seems to be finding a way to use developmental charts that acknowledge the concerns outlined. It seems therefore that developmental assessment needs to be used reflectively; and with a critical awareness of issues around their underpinning assumptions. And, if they are used critically and reflexively, (with an awareness of practitioners' own understandings and views), then developmental assessment is likely to be a more nuanced, personalised, relevant, and therefore more useful process.

C H A P T E R   S U M M A R Y

This chapter has developed the ideas from the last chapter, of questioning, analysing and evaluating what we know within the field of early years. It has outlined what is meant by a critical approach and given some examples of this approach with regard to particular issues in early years. One of the concepts that is critiqued is developmentalism, the topic of this book. The chapter highlights how the decontextualised nature of age/stage developmental trajectories is cause for concern. However, it recognises that alternatives to developmentalism are difficult to articulate as developmental psychology is powerfully embedded in our understandings of children and childhood. It also recognises that early years practitioners will be working within frameworks that adopt a developmental approach to children's learning, and therefore, a critically aware and reflexive approach is necessary to ensure that developmental assessment considers the child in a holistic way.

FURTHER READING

Allan, G (2011) *Early intervention. The next steps.* **www.dwp.gov.uk/docs/early-intervention-next-steps.pdf**

Baker, B (1999) The dangerous and the good? Developmentalism, progress and public schooling. *American Education Research Journal,* 36(4): 797–834.

Burman, E (2008) *Deconstructing developmental psychology.* London: Routledge.

Dahlberg, G, Moss, P and Pence, A (1999) *Beyond quality in early childhood and care. Postmodern perspectives.* London: Falmer Press.

DFE (2012) *Development Matters in the Early Years Foundation Stage.* **http://media.education.gov.uk/assets/files/pdf/d/development%20matters%20in%20the%20eyfs.pdf**

Field, F (2010) *The foundation years. Preventing poor children becoming poor adults.* **http://webarchive.nationalarchives.gov.uk/20110120090128/http://povertyreview.independent.gov.uk/media/20254/poverty-report.pdf**

Gilligan, C (1982) *In a different voice. Psychological theory and women's development.* London: Harvard University Press.

James, A and Prout, A (1997) *Constructing and reconstructing childhood. Contemporary issues in the sociological study of childhood.* London: Routledge Falmer.

Kohlberg, L (1973) The claim to moral adequacy of a highest stage of moral judgment. *Journal of Philosophy*, 70(18): 630–646.

Sheridan, M (2008) Revised and updated by Sharma J and Cockerill H (2008) *From birth to five*. London: Routledge.

References

Ainsworth, M and Bell, S (1970) Attachment, exploration and separation. *Child Development*, 41(1).

Aitchison, J (2008) *The articulate mammal*. Adingdon: Routledge.

Allan, G (2011) *Early intervention: the next steps*. **http://www.dwp.gov.uk/docs/early-intervention-next-steps.pdf**

Anning, A and Ball, M (2008) *Improving services for young children. From SureStart to children's centres.* London: Sage.

Athey, C (1990) *Extending thought in young children*. London: Paul Chapman.

Baker, B (1999) The dangerous and the good? Developmentalism, progress and public schooling. *American Education Research Journal*, 36 (4): 797–834.

Beaver, M (1994) *Babies and young children development 0–7*. Cheltenham: Nelson Thornes.

Bissex, G (1980) *GNYS AT WORK. A child learns to read and write*. Cambridge, MA: Harvard University Press.

Bolton, G (2005) *Reflective practice. Writing and professional development*. 2nd edition. London: Sage.

Borofsky, R (2005) *Yanomani: the fierce controversy and what we can learn from it.* University of California Press.

Boud, D, Keogh, R and Walker, D (1985) *Reflection: turning learning into experience*. London: Paul Chapman.

Bowlby, J (1953) *Child care and the growth of love*. London: Penguin.

Bretherton, I (1992) The origins of attachment theory: John Bowlby and Mary Ainsworth. *Developmental Psychology*, 28: 759–775. **http://www.psychology.sunysb.edu/attachment/online/inge_origins.pdf**

Broberg, AG (2000) A review of interventions in the parent-child relationship informed by attachment theory. *Acta Paediatrica*, 89: 37–42.

Brookfield, S (1990) Using critical incidents to explore leavers' assumptions, in J Mezirow and associates (eds) *Fostering critical reflection in adulthood.* San Francisco: Josey-Bass.

Bruce, T and Meggit, C (1999) *Childcare and education*. London: Hodder and Stoughton.

Burman, E (2008) *Deconstructing Developmental Psychology*. London: Routledge.

Carr, M (2001) *Assessment in early childhood settings: learning stories*. London: Sage.

Chagnon, N (1968) *Yanomamo. The fierce people.* New York: Holt Reinhart Winston.

Clark, A and Moss, P (2001) *Listening to young children*. London: National Children's Bureau.

Cunningham, H **http://open2.net/theinventionofchildhood/childhood_inventions.html**

Dahlberg, G, Moss, P, and Pence, P (1999) *Beyond quality in early childhood and care. Postmodern perspectives.* London: Falmer Books.

DCFS (2008) *Inclusion development programme. Supporting children with speech, language and communication needs: guidance for practitioners in the Early Years Foundation Stage*. DCFS Nottingham 00215–20008BKT-EN. **http://webarchive.nationalarchives.gov.uk/20110202093118/http:/nationalstrategies.standards.dcsf.gov.uk/ search/inclusion/results/nav:46335**

DCFS (2009) *Deprivation and education*. DCFS. **https://www.education.gov.uk/publications/standard/publicationDetail/Page1/DCSF-RTP-09–01**

DFE (2012) *Statutory Framework for the Early Years Foundation Stage*. DFE. **https://www.education.gov.uk/publications/standard/publicationDetail/Page1/DFE-00023–2012**

DFES (2001) *Special Educational Needs Code of Practice*. DFES. **https://www.education.gov.uk/publications/standard/publicationDetail/Page1/DfES%200581%202001**

DFE (2012) *Statutory Framework for the Early Years Foundation Stage*. DFE. **https://www.education.gov.uk/publications/standard/publicationDetail/Page1/DFE-00023–2012**

DFE (2012b) *Development matters in the Early Years Foundation Stage*. **http://media.education.gov.uk/assets/files/pdf/d/development%20matters%20in%20the%20eyfs.pdf**

Donaldson (1978) cited in Sutherland, P (1992) *Cognitive development today*. *Piaget and his critics*. London: Paul Chapman Press.

Drummond, MJ (1993) *Assessing children's learning*. London: David Fulton.

Empson, J and Nabuzoka, D with Hamilton, D (2004) *Atypical child development in context*. Basingstoke: Palgrave Macmillan.

Farrell, P and Ainscow, M (2002) *Making special education inclusive*. London: David Fulton Publishers.

Feinstein (2003) in DCFS (2009) Deprivation and Education. DCFS. **https://www.education.gov.uk/publications/standard/publicationDetail/Page1/DCSF-RTP-09–01**

Field, F (2010) *The foundation years. Preventing poor children becoming poor adults*. **http://webarchive.national archives.gov.uk/20110120090128/ http://povertyreview.independent.gov.uk/media/20254/poverty-report.pdf**

Gergen, K (1999) *An introduction to social constructionism*. London: Sage.

Gilligan, C (1982) *In a different voice. Psychological theory and women's development*. London: Harvard University Press.

Hart, B and Risley, T (1995) *Meaningful differences in the everyday experience of young American children*. London: Paul H Brookes Publishing.

Hirsch (2007) in DCFS (2009) Deprivation and Education. DCFS. **https://www.education.gov.uk/publications/standard/publicationDetail/Page1/DCSF-RTP-09–01**

Hobbs (2003) in DCFS (2009) Deprivation and Education. DCFS. **https://www.education.gov.uk/publications/standard/publicationDetail/Page1/DCSF-RTP-09–01**

James, A and Prout, A (1997) *Constructing and reconstructing childhood. Contemporary issues in the sociology study of childhood*. London: RoutledgeFalmer.

James, H, Sylva, K, Melhuish, E, Sammons, P, Siraj-Blatchford, I and Taggart, B (2009) The role of pre-school quality in promoting resilience in the cognitive development of young children. Oxford Review of Education 35(3): 331–352.

Jarman, E (2007) *Communication friendly spaces. Improving speaking and listening skills in the Early Years Foundation Stage*. Nottingham: Basic Skills Agency. **www.basic-skills.co.uk info@elizabethjarman.co.uk**

Jasper, M (2003) *Beginning reflective practice*. Cheltenham: Nelson Thornes.

Katz, L and Chard, S (1996) *The contribution of documentation to the quality of early childhood education.* http://www.cariboo.bc.ca/ae/literacies/reggio/reggioarticle1.htm

Kahn, T and Young, N (2007) *Embracing equality. Promoting equality and inclusion in the Early Years.* London: Pre-School Learning Alliance.

Kohlberg, L (1973) The claim to moral adequacy of a highest stage of moral judgment. *Journal of Philosophy*, 70(18): 630–646.

Layard, R and Dunn, J (2009) *A good childhood. Searching for values in a competitive age.* London: Penguin Books.

Livingston, J (1997) *Metacognition. An overview.* http://gse.buffalo.edu/fas/shuell/CEP564/Metacog.htm

Moss, P (2008) in Paige-Smith, A and Craft, A (2008) *Developing reflective practice in the early years.* Berkshire: Open University Press.

Moss, P and Petrie, P (2002) *From children's services to children's spaces: public policy, children and childhood.* London: RoutledgeFalmer.

Moyles, J (2005) *The excellence of play.* Maidenhead: Open University Press.

Neaum, S (2005) *Literacy, pedagogy and the early years.* Unpublished thesis. University of Nottingham.

Neaum, S (2012) *Language and literacy for the early years.* London: Sage.

Neaum, S and Tallack, J (1997) *Good practice in implementing the pre-school curriculum.* Cheltenham: Stanley Thornes.

Nutbrown, C (1999) *Threads of thinking. Young children learning and the role of early education.* London: Paul Chapman.

Nutbrown, C (2012) *Foundations for Quality. An independent review of early education and childcare qualifications.* www.education.gov.uk/nutbrownreview

Nutbrown, K and Clough, P (2006) *Inclusion in the early years.* London: Sage.

Piaget, J (2001) *The psychology of intelligence.* London: Routledge.

Prout, A (2005) *The future of childhood.* London: RoutledgeFalmer.

Reay (2006) in DCFS (2009) Deprivation and Education. DCFS. https://www.education.gov.uk/publications/standard/publicationDetail/Page1/DCSF-RTP-09–01

Reed, M and Canning, N (2009) *Reflective practice in the early years.* London: Sage.

Robinson, T (2005) *The worst children's jobs in history.* London: Pan.

Siraj-Blatchford, I, Sylva, K, Muttock, S, Gilden, R and Bell D (2002) *Researching effective pedagogy in the early years (REPEY).* Research Report RR356. DCFS. http://www.dfes.gov.uk/research/data/uploadfiles/RR356.pdf

Skelton, C, Francis, B and Valkanova, Y (2007) *Breaking down the stereotypes. Gender and achievement in schools.* Equal Opportunities Commission Working paper number 59 www.equalityhumanrights.com/en/publicationsandresources/gender/pages/research.aspx

Social Exclusion Task Force (2008) in DCFS (2009) Deprivation and Education. DCFS. https://www.education.gov.uk/publications/standard/publicationDetail/Page1/DCSF-RTP-09–01

Sylva, K and Pugh, G (2005) Transforming the Early Years in England. *Oxford Review of Education* 31 (1): 11–27.

Sylva, K, Meluish, E, Sammons, P, Siraj-Blatchford, I, Taggart, B and Elliot, K (2003) *Effective Provision of Pre-School (EPPE) Project: findings from the pre-school period.* **http://eppe.ioe.ac.uk/eppe/eppefindings.htm**

Tough, J (1976) *Listening to children talking.* East Grinstead: Ward Locke.

Waddell, M (1992) *Owl babies.* London: Walker Books.

Washbrook, E and Waldfogel, J (2010) *Low income and early cognitive development in the UK.* The Sutton Trust. **http://www.suttontrust.com/annualreports.asp**

Index

Added to a page number 't' denotes a table and 'f' a figure.